ROAMING THE LABYRINTH

with **MARIE-CLAIRE BANCQUART**

Poems, Prose & Translations
CHRISTINA COOK

Roaming the Labyrinth with Marie-Claire Bancquart: Poems, Prose & Translations
First Edition 2025 © Christina Cook
French originals © Marie-Claire Bancquart, reprinted by kind
permission of the publishers listed in the acknowledgments (p. 211)

Published in the United States of America by
AIM Higher, Inc.
West Hurley, New York

ISBN
979-8-9863699-4-5 (Hardcover)
979-8-9863699-5-2 (Paperback)

Library of Congress Control Number: 2025931150

Book design: Shanna Compton
Copy editor, English: Cindy Hochman, "100 Proof" Copyediting Services
Copy editor, French: Amanda Sarasien

Back cover poem: "Sunday Spaces" trans. by Christina Cook

Cover art: *Within the Labyrinth*, digital collage created with public
domain sources: *Mazes and Labyrinths: A General Account of Their
History and Developments*, W. H. Matthews (Longmans, Green & Co.,
1922) and "En Rose," Michael Fosie, engraving (1740–1749)

Ordering & Contact
do@aimhigher.org

Praise for *Roaming the Labyrinth with Marie-Claire Bancquart*

Poets know how privileged they are to be translated by like-minded poets. Christina Cook's accomplished translations of French poet Marie-Claire Bancquart are among the most sensual and nuanced versions I've encountered. But *Roaming the Labyrinth with Marie-Claire Bancquart* is more than a work of translation presented bilingually: it is an original work of hybrid writing, rich in its sources, narratives, extrapolations, and more. "In my poetry and my personal life, Marie-Claire taught me to *engage* with my disbelief rather than suspend it," writes Cook as she gracefully weaves her autobiographical prose and poetry through a well-curated selection of Bancquart's poems in translation. Voices, images, histories, timespaces multiply, dialoguing with one another against the backdrop of Paris, music, mythology ... This generous work celebrates the joyful union of writing and translation and pays homage to an enduring friendship between two women, born of a "language of desire" *deep in the body*.
—**Fiona Sze-Lorrain**

Christina Cook's *Roaming the Labyrinth with Marie-Claire Bancquart* blends literary criticism, memoir, and travelogue into a poignant and integrated whole. The framing story is Cook's one day and evening in Paris with writer Marie-Claire Bancquart and her husband, composer Alain Bancquart. Exquisite prose is enlivened with poems by Marie-Claire and Christina, making a book that honors the making of art.
—**Natasha Sajé**, author of *Terroir: Love, Out of Place*

Part memoir, part biography, part translation, part poetry—Christina Cook has created an enthralling hybrid text that gives an intimate glimpse of a major French poet and her influence on the author. The pairing of Bancquart's poems with Cook's own poetry is especially illuminating, as it shows how accomplished she is at capturing Bancquart's voice rather than bending it through her own prism. I hope readers of English will fall in love with Bancquart through this book.

—**Wendeline A. Hardenberg,** translator of *With Death,*
an Orange Segment Between Our Teeth,
poems by Marie-Claire Bancquart

For Marie-Claire and Alain

Contents

Author's Note on the Music

Marie-Claire Bancquart and her husband, composer Alain Bancquart, collaborated on several musical pieces together. One of them, a microtonal oratorio titled *Livre du Labyrinthe*, is quoted and referred to throughout this book. The piece was performed at Radio France's Salle Olivier Messiaen in 2000. The recording of it (Mode Records 120/21 (2-CDs), 2008) can be found at https://moderecords.com/catalog/120_121bancquart/. It can also be found on all major streaming platforms, Naxos Music Library, and Alexander Street Music Online: Classical Music Library.

I highly recommend listening to this otherworldly and wildly original music while reading poems from and inspired by it, especially Marie-Claire's poem "Minotaure" and my poem "Driving Through Shrouds." In the CD liner notes, Alain describes *Livre du Labyrinthe* as "neither an opera nor a suite of instrumental and vocal pieces. We would like it to be a walk through a myth, inside a mythical garden—particularly like that of the baroque park of Bomarzo in Italy which is populated by statues of monsters."

Listen to the Bancquarts' garden gate creak open as you turn this page.

Prologue

Nos paupières fermées | Our Eyelids Closed

IMAGINE YOUR BODY stretched out on a metal bed, immobile because your outermost layer of skin is actually a plaster cast. Sanatorium nurses wheel you outside on warm days. Sometimes they read to you, but more often they just leave you for hours to ponder your existence. Lying flat on your back gives you a peculiar perspective, something akin to the way a meadow, lake, or large slab of stone might see the world. After five years, you begin to feel like your material makeup is essentially a meadow, lake, or large slab of stone. You see countless birds going from the air above to the far-off trees. You close your eyes; wonder if you can see their reflection inside your body. You can. You wonder if their flapping is in fact the pulse of your relentless pain. At twelve years old, you've spent nearly half your life like this: it is the only existence you remember. Death is on your mind because children all around you are dying of the same disease as you. Because it is World War II, and birds aren't the only things flying through French skies.

Au profond du corps

Nos paupières fermées
le regard au profond du corps
voit des oiseaux sans nombre
qui vont des poumons aux cellules lointaines

nous nous étirons
dans le resserrement de notre peau

nous devenons
un arbre, ciel compris

nous soutenons l'oiseau.

Deep in the Body

Eyelids closed
our look deep in the body
sees countless birds
going from lungs to far-off cells

we stretch
in our skin's constriction

become
a tree, sky included

we hold the bird up.

MARIE-CLAIRE BANCQUART (née Chauvet) was born in 1932 in the coal-mining town of Aubin, France. World War II and skeletal tuberculosis prevented her from attending elementary school, but her spacious interior world provided seeds of deep thought that would eventually bloom into more than thirty collections of poetry, six novels, and well over seventy critical texts: an oeuvre that would earn her a place as one of the most important figures in turn-of-the-twenty-first-century French literature.

In 1955, Bancquart received her *agrégation* in Classical Literature from l'École normale supérieure de Sèvres. The degree prepared her for an illustrious teaching career, with professorships at the Universities of Brest, Rouen, Créteil, Nanterre, and lastly the Paris Sorbonne, where she became professor emerita. 1955 also saw her marriage to Alain Bancquart, a music student who would go on to become a highly lauded composer, professor at the National Conservatory, and musical director of the National Orchestra of France.

In July 2005, I had the pleasure of interviewing Marie-Claire at her Paris home for my MFA thesis. Little did I know when I scheduled the interview with this intimidatingly acclaimed poet that she and her husband would dedicate the day to showing me their favorite places around Paris, that this day would be an inflection point in my growth as a poet and a person—and the start of a profoundly special friendship.

In February 2019, I sent Marie-Claire an email, one of many we'd exchanged since 2005, but on this occasion it was Alain who responded: his wife, best friend, and creative collaborator of sixty-four years had passed away.

S'éclate

Avec la mort quartier d'orange entre les dents
on a voyagé dormi

soudain son jus
a giclé dans la bouche

l'été
s'éclate en alchimie

le soleil darde un œil couleur de fruit
sur notre temps qui tombe.

Revels

With death an orange slice between our teeth
we traveled asleep

suddenly its juice
spurted into our mouth

the summer
revels in alchemy

the sun shoots a fruit-colored glance
at our time which comes.

THE IMAGE of disembodied dead holding a juicy orange slice between their teeth is an important one for Marie-Claire, uniting the concrete and the abstract in a way that runs through her work. Moreover, "An orange segment is something *très agréable* to think about," she once told me. "Will the reader also find that death, in the end, is not just a negative thing [but rather a positive one in that it] brings us much closer to the animals, plants, and all things on Earth?"

The reason Bancquart finds death so, well, *pleasant* is that it closes the gap—she calls it *l'intervalle*—between the speaking thinking human body and other bodies layered into its landscape.

She championed the ancient Greek theory of atomism, which she described to me as "the idea that the human body is no more than a system of atoms which formed like many other systems of atoms and will, after death, disperse and cease to autonomously exist." Lucretius, a leading proponent of the theory, was in many ways a man 2,000 years before his time. If he reincarnated in this century (and who's to say he hasn't!), he'd surely be fascinated to find atomism's parallel in quantum theory, which as we know posits similar behavior in subatomic particles.

The consciousness that animates the temporary coherence of a human body compels us to express ourselves through language, which for Marie-Claire Bancquart both levies a wedge between us and the rest of the natural world and also provides our only means of expressing our physical connection to it. Bancquart's female gaze inside and outside the body creates a silent internal-external dialogue[1] which her poetry expresses in concrete images. Abstract language will not do. As Jean Cocteau writes in *The Art of Cinema*, "The closer you get to a mystery, the more important it is to be realistic."[2]

Bancquart's conception is very different from Rainer Maria Rilke's early "object poems" or his later works of existential materialism; different from William Carlos Williams's dictum that poetry should have "no ideas but in things," which became the mantra of twentieth-century Imagism. In the limelight of an "object poem" or Imagist poem, ordinary things become luminous; transcendent, even. In the more astringent—let's call it lemonlight—of a Bancquart poem, no such spiritual alchemy takes place between poet and object. What you see is what you get.

Du poète

La mort la vie :
équivoques.

Dans leur ombre
un larron dérobe les mots
les suractive

cris de joie et meurtres
parcourent la table
où la très belle femme en cire
sourit, le ventre ouvert sur ses entrailles
en
ostentation multicolore
de
fraises, poivrons, cerises.

Concerning the Poet

Death life:
ambiguous.

In their shadow
a thief steals the words
supercharges them:

screams of glee and murders
roam the table
where the gorgeous wax-woman
smiles, stomach open to entrails
in
multicolored ostentation
of
strawberries, sweet peppers, cherries.

BANCQUART HAS SAID that for a poet to express obscure ideas in even more obscure language is simply not "a good project. At least not for me," asserting that any poet who mistrusts the concrete image will invariably "ooze toward sentimental or false."[3]

Dear reader, I am living proof of the truth of this statement.

I became completely enamored with the poetry of William Wordsworth from the moment my mother opened the daffodil-bedecked two-page spread in *A Child's Book of Poems*[4] featuring "I Wandered Lonely as a Cloud." As I began exploring the craft of poetry, I stumbled over these lonely Wordsworth clouds—I sought a means to express my poetic intent without drifting away in them on my path to clarify my own poetic voice. The hundreds, if not thousands, of hours I went on to spend translating Marie-Claire's poetry have been important steps on that path, supercharged by hearing novelist Antonine Maillet speak at an American Literary Translators Association conference.

Maillet asserted that the translator's job is to begin translating a text at the precise point the original writer began writing it. The translator must, like the writer, begin at the point where there was no text, then create the very same text in the target language that the original writer created in the source language.

Experimenting with Maillet's advice, I found that tracing the essence of Marie-Claire's poems did yield an experience of actually writing them. I learned, by doing, to employ prosody that was both wildly creative and almost mathematically precise. I learned to relegate adjectives and adverbs to the top of the word pyramid, to be used as sparingly as the fats, oils, and sweets that top the USDA food pyramid. I learned to use clever neologisms and choose words rare but not archaic. I learned to employ elliptical syntax and irregular punctuation, mismatch verb conjugations to their subjects, and omit key parts of speech. As the poet of these English-language lines, I saw how all these linguistic gymnastics created space for a reader to collaborate in the meaning-making process of the poem. As the translator of the French lines, I saw the critical importance of disregarding the meanings I'd personally made of the poems in order to create the same collaborative space for Anglophone readers that Marie-Claire had so generously created for her Francophone audience.

I also learned to write poems from Marie-Claire's atheist perspective, which challenged my then-Christian beliefs—though, truth be told, those were already on shaky ground. My mother's ongoing suffering from metastatic breast cancer, despite my desperate pleas to God, felt like the final straw in the series of assaults to her autonomy and dignity that she'd endured over the course of her life under the patriarchal weight of the Catholic Church. When Marie-Claire voiced her perspective during our day together, her words resonated with me more strongly than church bells:

> God is said to be good, but the moment violence appears, God disappears. It is the same with illness. When I was very sick as a child, I saw death up close, as did the other children who were sick like me. How could "God" let this happen? Nothing accounts for a good God, so people imagine one, create one. This is why from the time I was young, though I received some religious instruction, I never believed in God.

Translating Marie-Claire's poetry at a time of profound personal, spiritual, intellectual, and poetic growth layered my efforts with complexity and depth in a way that had an indelible impact on me. This is not to say I went on to become a mini-Marie-Claire—nor would she have wanted that. My poetry is distinctly different from hers, as is my worldview. Though no longer a member of any religious institution, neither am I an atheist. But after spending an intense period of time translating *her* poetry, a discernible shift occurred in *mine*: I began to demand more from it. I began to see how my own poetry had been constrained by a hidden adherence to the cultural perspective that ghosted through the

English language. I began to see a poem's framework as the spacious mat of a gymnast's floor routine rather than a balance beam.

So, too, did I see Bancquart's use of mythological narratives infused with the same spaciousness and refusal to toe the line. Laying creative claim to received myths—which all of us own—is exactly what another of my mentors, poet Clare Rossini, had been encouraging me to do. Instead of writing poems about the antiquated storylines that were passed down to us, she encouraged me to approach them in novel ways that reveal new perspectives and possibilities. After all, the only way to challenge out-moded assumptions trapped in the canon of Western culture's "received wisdom" is to diversify the spectrum of the voices.

Clare opened the door. Marie-Claire invited me inside. I set about translating poems such as "And Counterfable of Eurydice." To recap the myth to which the poem alludes: Hades, king of the Underworld, grants Orpheus's request to lead his beloved Eurydice back into the world of the living, but on the condition that he not turn around to see her . . . which of course he does, dooming her to spend eternity in the Underworld. The traditional telling of the myth—which is to say, the telling of it through a normative male perspective—assumes that Eurydice is as devastated about it as Orpheus is. Bancquart's retelling suggests otherwise.

Et contrefable d'Eurydice

Le gonflement du miel
quand il m'embrassait pénétrait mon corps.

Lions et lièvres
baissaient leurs cils avec les miens.

Mais le dieu d'outre-sang
a délicieusement gelé mon paysage.

Pris dans la vitre il déroulait
pour toujours la fleur de ses notes.

Orphée le prédateur va devant moi
restaure à chaque pas les cils prêts à tomber
le corps en usure de sang
la peau tiède et ternie d'Eurydice voguant en vieillesse.

J'écarte désormais moiteur exil mûrissement.

J'appelle cet échange interdit de regards
pour retrouver
non le visage de l'amour
mais celui du destin qui m'exaltait dans le mica des mortes.

And Counterfable of Eurydice

The swelling of the honey
when he kissed me penetrated my body.

Lions and hares
lowered their lashes with mine.

But the god beyond blood
deliciously froze my landscape.

Caught in the rolled-up window
forever the flower of his notes.

Orpheus the predator goes before me
restores with each step the eyelashes ready to fall
the blood-worn body
the tepid tarnished skin of Eurydice wandering in old age.

I dismiss moisture exile ripening.

I name this forbidden exchange of looks
to retrieve
not the face of love

but that of the destiny which exalted me in the mica of the dead.

THROUGHOUT HER POETRY and fiction, Bancquart reinvents many mythic characters' journeys or perspectives in order to breathe expansive new life into their ancient archetypes. For example, in her novel *Les tarots d'Ulysse*, no sooner does Ulysses finally return to Ithaca than he leaves again, this time, she told me, "in order to fulfill his god-mandated destiny to die, showing himself to be not only a mythical hero, but every bit as mortal as you and I." And in her lyrics to Alain's opus *Livre du Labyrinthe*, the hero Theseus physically becomes one with the monstrous Minotaur. So, too, in her poem "Icare," does Icarus plummet to his death only to "prepare his arrival in the English rose," whose deep red blossoms open millennia later.

In my poetry and my personal life, Marie-Claire taught me to *engage* with my disbelief rather than suspend it. This, in turn, empowered me to refashion archetypal myths into narratives that empower female characters to go on their own journeys of self-discovery and world-discovery—rather than being silenced, raped, or transformed into trees, reeds, or stars to avoid being raped.

In translating Marie-Claire's poems and coming to know her as an incredible—and incredibly kind and generous—force of nature, I've learned that such magic is mine for the taking. That words, especially potent when poetic, are pure magic. Whenever I need to be reminded of this, I take out my Tarot deck and find *Le Bateleur,* The Magician, whose words, they say, have the power to bend reality.

Tarot

I.

L'escamoteur figure en tête du destin
Jouant aux gobelets
Son propre corps

Il feint d'en étaler le jeu sur une planche
À l'usage de qui voudrait

sa bouche
vers le feu du ciel
ses ongles ses cheveux avec les crinières des bêtes

N'y croyez pas
Son chapeau d'infini
c'est
dans ses veines

La véritable création
charriant des gestes en grappe
au milieu des poumons
dirige son index vers la dérive du silence.

Tarot

I. The Magician

The conjurer figures in the head of destiny
Playing cups
His own body

He pretends to lay the game out on a board
For anyone who fancies

his mouth
toward the sky's fire
his nails his hair with the manes of beasts

Don't believe it
His infinity hat
is
in his veins

The true creation
carrying gestures in clusters
in the middle of his lungs
directs his index finger toward the derivation of silence.

IN BANCQUART'S MIND, the Magician's *real* connection to infinity isn't his infinity-symbol hat, but rather the infinite loop of blood circulating through his veins. Moreover, the formation of words in his lungs is what gives him his *real* creative power. Marie-Claire is every bit the *Bateleur*, bending reality into an arc of unvarnished truth that enters and exits our lungs in what she describes as "a concrete respiration that encompasses us all . . . men, animals, plants, stones, stars."[5]

In 2022, Alain too died, joining Marie-Claire in this concrete respiration and leaving me to roam the labyrinth of our special bond alone. In my mind, the memory of our daylong journey through Paris took on a magical life of its own: one rife with the work of the *Bateleur* and her mythical entourage.

Chapter One

Remontant un fil du monde | Rewinding a Thread of the World

I EMERGE FROM THE MÉTRO tunnels into the dark air of Paris. The moment unspools in slow motion: gold statues, Rococo facades, slithering Seine, French language lapping at my ears.

I hail a taxi and sink into the driver's Arabian dance music as he ferries me to my fin-de-siècle hotel in the 16th arrondissement. The next morning, I rise early and take my Tarot deck out onto the balconette. I draw a card, as I do every morning, not to divine my day's fortune but rather to get a sense of the landscape I'll be navigating. I've drawn the Hermit, suggesting reclusiveness—odd for the interactive day ahead of me. On second thought, maybe not so odd. After all, navigating an inner landscape doesn't necessitate physical isolation. And I'll certainly be spending time discussing *le profond du corps* with Marie-Claire. Moreover, the Hermit's skill at interpreting clues and symbols will come in handy—if even just to find my way to her apartment. I slip the card into my purse for extra measure. After a croissant and coffee in the hotel's quiet inner courtyard, I step out onto the sidewalk. I'm stepping into a Bancquart poem.

My first order of business is to find a flower shop en route to Marie-Claire's. Only several steps along, though, and the song of a swallow-tailed kite distracts me. Enchanted, I turn down a narrow cobblestone alley— so narrow, I'm not entirely sure if the path is a public one. Aside from the siren song of this bird that's said to be, like Hermes, a messenger between worlds, the streets are silent. No one's around. So I walk deeper in. The alley leads to a lush pocket park with a large fountain in the center: River nymphs are frolicking with fish, out of whose mouths burble gentle jets of water. Two elderly women startle up at me from their bench, causing a ball of thread to fall off one of their laps and roll several meters away. I rush over to collect it, then wind it back up for them, apologizing for my intrusion and complimenting the red scarf they're knitting, one at each end.

"Je cherche un fleuriste et j'ai peur de me perdre," I say. "Y en a-t-il un à proximité?"

One of the women suggests I snip stems off the rosebushes behind them instead of buying flowers at a shop. The other eyes her disapprovingly. I eventually secure directions to two local flower shops, each woman favoring a different one. They point me past the dark red rosebushes and down a peastone path that opens into a large public garden. Market stalls are set up at the far end of it, and as I walk nearer, I see them spilling into side streets as well. I pass wooden crates of oranges and plump purple figs. Baskets of pineapples and mangoes. Carrots, zucchini, and cucumbers piled in tidy rows. Heads of jewel-green kale and chard. All of it glistens with wetness.

Millénaires

L' homme, ce tard venu, remonte un fil du monde
côtoyant les étals de primeurs

cageots, palettes du marché
sentent, mouillés, leur arbre d'origine.

Vers le tréfonds de nous
transfusion
des millénaires moisissures
troncs, herbes
sous la montée des eaux.

La douce chair, la tourbe acide se rejoignent
sur ce bord de trottoir urbain
éclaboussé par les voitures.

Millennial

Mankind, this late in coming, rewinds a thread of the world
along the stalls of produce

crates, market pallets
smell, wet, like their tree of origin.

Toward our depths
transfusion
of millennial mold
trunks, grasses
beneath the rising of the waters.

The sweet flesh, acidic peat blend
on this urban curbside
splattered by cars.

THE STREET MARKET through which I thread seems mysteriously similar to the one Bancquart conjures in her poem. I can even see her sweeping vision of humankind's umbilical connection to its preexistence on earth. When I translated "Millennial," I realized that its mythopoetic flavor comes from the unique combination of what the poem lacks (a fluid narrative, familiar punctuation, any reference to people in a clearly peopled scene) and what it contains (concrete objects and sensory images). Like many of her poems, it remains firmly grounded in the very place and time it transcends.

I continue to think about "Millennial" as I wind my way through the market stalls, keeping an eye out for a flower vendor. I think about the myth of Theseus and the Minotaur—one of Marie-Claire's and my favorites—and imagine Ariadne sending Theseus into a labyrinth with her ball of thread to find fresh produce rather than slay a beast. I imagine Theseus unwinding his way out again, arms loaded with oranges, figs, heirloom tomatoes; imagine him unspooling himself out the labyrinth of market stalls and into his inner one, where the cells of his body transfuse with the primordial swish of spores and grasses in the waters that once filled the Paris Basin. Here, the hero can merge with the beast in his body's depths. Here, in the bowels of Paris, far beneath the catacombs, beneath the fossil-riddled bedrock, in a place of original darkness. The labyrinth's perfection.

Minotaure

(Récitant)
Le Minotaure rêve. Il cherche. Il brûle. Il croit se changer en navire.
Il touche au royaume
où il retrouve
les gens d'outre-mémoire ;
son père le taureau, Dédale, qui serra les murs autour de lui.

Voici que le fil parvient à son corps.
Il s'éveille. Il jette les yeux sur Thésée.
C'est le premier, parmi les hommes, à ne pas mourir sous son regard.

Il le voit brandir un poignard. Il sent la mort enfoncer une pointe
jusqu'au plus noir de sa poitrine.
Fulgurance de la blessure
douleur
c'est la première qu'il ressent.
Il pleure le déchirement du passage vers l'autre rive.
Lui, le solaire, le violent,
quelque chose l'unit désormais aux larmes des sapins
aux blessures des peuples, aux abattoirs
et l'unit
aux chairs juteuses des fruits qu'il ne connaît pas, à la douceur des rivières.
Inondé de sanglots
sachant les suintements, les pertes,
il tombe.
Par terre, se dessinent à plat, bien précis, les contours de son mufle
de bête et de son corps humain.

Cri dernier, sourd oracle de deuil, cri de naissance aussi.

Homme de nuit comme de jour, bête désirante et désappointée,
il a maintenant parcouru son destin. Il peut entrer dans les territoires
qui ne connaissaient pas d'autre mur que le vent,
d'autre porte que la grande mer.
Il y entre d'un seul bond délivré. Plus d'obstacle !

(Thésée)(en même temps que le dernier texte du récitant)
Goutte à goutte le sang
coule de mon poignard.
Ce sang contre ma peau
ce sang qui passe
ma frontière de peau, et pénètre mon sang.

Le Minotaure
transfuse en moi.

Il monte lentement l'échelle de mon corps.
Tout s'entrechoque.
Je ne connais plus le brouillard des meurtres, la tristesse des pleurs.

Pour la première fois vient ce sourire
tellement nouveau
que je le cache entre mes mains.

(Récitant)
Et ses doigts peu à peu sentent qu'ils n'enserrent plus un visage.
Poil doux. Mufle de Minotaure
Bonheur d'être animal avec des mains humaines.
Le Thésée-Minotaure écarte ses doigts. Devant lui, un faux Thésée
commence à rembobiner le fil noir. Il lui tend son poignard. Adieu,
guerrier triste, adieu, simulacre, qui le remplacera chez les hommes !

Quant à lui, lentement couché auprès du Minotaure mort, il l'étreint.
Il se confond, fils de la pluie et du sourire, avec ce fils du soleil et des
larmes. L'un à l'autre, ils se sont donné la perfection du labyrinthe.

The Minotaur

(Narrator)
The Minotaur dreams. He seeks. He burns. He thinks he's turning
into a ship.
He encounters the kingdom
where he finds
people from beyond memory;
his father the bull; Daedalus, who cinched the walls in around him.

Here the thread reaches his body.
He awakes. He glares at Theseus,
first among men to survive his gaze.

He sees Theseus brandish a dagger. He feels death drive a blade
into the darkest part of his chest.
Lightning strike of a wound
pain
he first feels.
He deplores being wrenched across to the other shore.
He, the solar, the violent, now
something merges him with the fir trees' tears
with people's wounds, slaughterhouses
mixed with
the juicy flesh of unknown fruits, rivers' sweetness.
Awash with tears
aware of the leaching, the losses,
he falls.
On the ground, the outline of his beast-muzzle and man-body
takes two-dimensional shape.
Death cry, dull oracle of mourning, birth cry too.

Man by night as by day, desiring and disappointed beast, he's now
roamed the whole of his destiny. He can enter landscapes
whose only walls are wind, whose only door is the open sea.
He enters in a single bound. No more obstacles!

(Theseus) (sung along with the above text of the narrator)
Drop by drop the blood
drips from my dagger.
This blood against my skin
this blood that crosses
my skin's border, and penetrates my blood.

The Minotaur
transfuses into me.

He slowly climbs the ladder in my body.
Everything converges.
I no longer know the fog of murder, the sadness of tears.

For the first time comes this smile
So new
I couch it in my hands.

(Narrator)
Little by little, his fingers no longer feel they're clenching a face.
Soft coat. Minotaur muzzle
Happiness of an animal with human hands.

The Theseus-Minotaur splays his fingers. Before him, a fake Theseus
begins rewinding the black thread, hands him the dagger. Farewell,
sad warrior, farewell, simulacrum, who will replace him among men!

The real Theseus slowly lies down beside the dead Minotaur,
embraces him. Son of rain and smiles merges with son of sun and tears.
One to the other, they've given each other the perfection of the labyrinth.

IT IS THE FAKE THESEUS, then, the cad who has not integrated his inner beast, who winds his way out of the labyrinth and soon after abandons Ariadne on the island of Naxos. In some versions of the myth, Ariadne hangs herself in despair, but in most accounts, Bacchus, the god of wine and pleasure, falls in love with her. When they marry, Bacchus tosses her wedding diadem up into the heavens, where it remains to this day as the constellation Corona Borealis. In *Bacchus and Ariadne*, Titian's color-rich rendering of this scene, Ariadne stands at the water's edge wearing an indigo-blue robe over a white tunic. A long red scarf encircles her torso and limbs.

A heady scent telescopes my mind back into my immediate surroundings. I find myself standing right outside *un magasin de farces et attrapes*, a joke shop, and beside that is the flower shop that one of the women suggested to me. Roses of every kind and color fill the umbrellaed storefront. Purple, red, pink, and mauve roses fill one tin bucket. Large white roses, spray roses, and pussy willows fill another. Potted roses climb up awning poles, red roses sit cinched into heart-shaped table arrangements. I select a bouquet and hand it to the florist. While she wraps it in crisp white paper, a couple walks in. Astonishment: the woman is wearing a white evening gown with a loose bodice gathered Greekly over one shoulder. Encircling her waist, arms, and neck is a long red scarf. It seems to me the very same one the women were knitting in the park this morning. The man she's with is maned with long curly red hair and clad in a dress shirt the same color as his olive skin. A dusty pink tie has been loosed from around his neck. He's a bit off-kilter, perhaps drunk, perhaps simply strange. The woman is sober and elegant. She has an air of folly about her. From a bucket, he plucks a bouquet of three dozen red roses, lays cash on the counter, then leaves with the woman. The florist hands me my bouquet, which now seems puny by comparison. I pay her and leave the shop, stopping to watch the couple walk away. They disappear into the vanishing point of my sight line, streetlamps flickering out behind them. The moon hovers indecisively above.

Du dimanche

Je ne sais pas si je t'écris
un poème d'amour

aussi bien je le dédierais aux espaces du dimanche

le nuage roule
dans des fenêtres inconnues
de la ville parcourue et reparcourue

étonnement :
marcher, nous deux,
sous les réverbères irréguliers
tout au long des Tarots, allant du Bateleur au Fou.

La promenade
est-elle d'amour, ou de connivence au plus vaste que nous ?

Sunday Spaces

I don't know if I'm writing you
a love poem

I may as well dedicate it to Sunday spaces

the cloud drifts
in windows unknown
to the roamed and re-roamed city

astonishment:
to walk, we two,
below haphazard streetlamps
all along the Tarots, going from the Magician to the Fool.

Is the walk
one of love, or complicity in a vaster plan?

I'M REMINDED of Bancquart's novel *Les tarots d'Ulysse*, which imagines Ulysses leaving Ithaca for a second epic journey: one in which he reincarnates through a progression of Tarot figures ranging from the Magician, the Lovers, the Wheel of Fortune, Death, and the Tower to, finally, the Fool. And like the Tarot's Fool, who is always accompanied by a dog, Ulysses is reunited with the ghost of his faithful Argos at the close of the novel. Tarot cards—which arrived in Europe via the Silk Road in the fifteenth century—capture archetypal aspects of the human psyche with as much force as mythic figures; however, relatively few poets and literary novelists have made use of them.

My mind wanders back to my own Tarot draw that morning. I pull the Hermit out of my purse. I'm struck by the figure's resemblance to Ulysses when disguised as an old beggar upon his return to Ithaca. Like Ulysses, the Hermit represents the quintessence of resourceful practicality. After all, their archetypal journeys—and ours—are nothing if not purposeful. Nothing if not replete with twists and turns to find the ultimate unity that lies at our center. St. Teresa of Ávila called it her "interior castle." Dag Hammarskjöld saw it as "the wonder: that *I* exist." To Buddha it was "nirvana." For Marie-Claire, it is "the great nothing."

Tarot

VIIII.

Mais toi plus seul encore
aux portes mortelles

Un vieil empire
domestiqué :
tu veilles
avec mémoire de serpent

Tu sais que vague et flamme ont mêmes courbes annulées
dans les profondeurs du grand rien

Tel héritage
Tel improbable point de géomètre
Tu ne partages pas.

Mais ta graine amasse en secret
De quoi
s'insurger
en arbre.

Tarot

VIIII. The Hermit

But you're even more alone
at the mortal gates

An old empire
domesticated:
you watch
with snake memory

You know wave and flame have the same canceled curves
in the depths of the great nothing

Such heritage
Such unlikely surveyor's mark
You don't share.

But your seed secretly amasses
what's
rising up
via tree.

SEVERAL *PÂTÉS DE MAISONS* LATER, I am standing at an old glass and wood-paneled door wedged between a small market and a cozy-looking Lebanese restaurant. The merchant looks up from arranging ruler-straight rows of melons in their wooden cartons and tips his cap to me. I press the button beside the name "Bancquart," and Marie-Claire greets me over the intercom before buzzing me in. The foyer floor is laid with Carrara marble tiles. Its walls are paneled in dark oak; I peer into the panels' polished grain. My Hermit fingers feel the smooth surface of what once was sheathed in bark. My Hermit self sees secret seeds of rebellion there. I walk over to the elevator, not much bigger than a coffin. I pull aside its metal gate, then open its wooden gate and step inside, clanging each one shut behind me.

Chapter Two

Jasant par une fenêtre ouverte | Chatting by an Open Window

MARIE-CLAIRE IS WEARING a long skirt and a loose floral blouse. A triple-stranded choker and close-cropped red hair frame the delicate features of her face. She invites me into their spacious hallway and introduces me to her husband, Alain.

Alain has a high forehead and crown of fine white hair. A pair of prominent white eyebrows eagle his brown eyes. He's wearing slate-gray dress pants and a light gray button-down shirt. His smile is as warm as Marie-Claire's.

I present her with the bouquet and we exchange pleasantries. Then Marie-Claire suggests we get started with the interview. Her cat, Argos, a small piebald with a confident stride, trots ahead of us down the hall's parquet floor and into her study. I reach down to pet him, but he shies away. Marie-Claire arranges the roses in a crystal vase, complimenting their fragrance, and sets the arrangement on a plant stand beside her desk. She opens the French windows, whisking in the buzz of Parisian life below. Books line one whole wall; each shelf holds a double row of them. They are uniformly bound in thick ecru laid paper, all with unillustrated covers that feature little more than the book title in an elegant font—the trademark appearance of French literary publishing houses. Though Marie-Claire is walking with discomfort, she insists I take her upholstered desk chair while she sits down on a metal chair with a thin brown corduroy cushion. Argos stretches up from the floor to place his front paws on Marie-Claire's knee. He noses around the air until she strokes his back, then returns his paws to the floor and leaps onto her desk. He settles on his haunches, his face a foot away from mine, and stares at me. I reach over to pat his head, but he dodges me and turns in sudden fascination to the rose-colored curtains fluttering in the breeze. Marie-Claire chuckles and smooths her skirt.

I ask if Argos minds being named after a dog.

She laughs. "Pas du tout."

We start talking about her cat's namesake, Ulysses's loyal dog, then move on to ancient Greece. I ask her what Greek writers and philosophers most influenced her, both as a poet and one-time Classics student. Marie-Claire cites Virgil and Ovid, emphasizing the latter "because he came up with the idea of the continual metamorphosis of the universe—and depicted it extremely well in literature. For example," she says, "the story of Daphne's transformation into a laurel tree to avoid being violated by Apollo, who was pursuing her: when Apollo touched the trunk of the tree, he felt her heart still beating beneath the bark. This story touches me with particular strength because it shows the intimate closeness we have to the world."

Métamorphosés

Animaux taillés dans les buis
des villas proches de Venise.

Si nous étions les buis d'une divinité
sculptés avec tendresse, au ciseau doux ?

Le sombre à l'intérieur de nous
sortirait en feuilles minimes
        serrées
        d'odeur profonde.

Pareils aux métamorphosés d'Ovide, nous serions oublieux
des amours, des poursuites.

Auréolés d'air qui tremble au soleil

vers le soir
quand l'humidité monte sous un ciel vert
nous sentirions nos cœurs
rebattre un peu au milieu de nos branches

avec celui
des gens en trompe-l'œil aux fresques de la salle
jasant par la fenêtre ouverte
en mots légers, loin de l'aigreur des choses.

Metamorphoses

Animals of pruned boxwoods
in villa gardens near Venice.

If we were a god's boxwoods
sculpted tenderly, with gentle shears?

The dark inside us
would drop off in tiny leaves
                     dense
                     deep-odored.

As in Ovid's metamorphoses, we'd be forgetful
of loves, pursuits.

Haloed by air that trembles in the sun

toward evening
when fog rises under a green sky
we'd feel our hearts faintly
beat again amid our branches

with the heart
of folk in the villa's trompe l'oeil frescoes
chatting by an open window
with light words, far from the bitterness of things.

MARIE-CLAIRE TELLS ME she wrote this poem after a trip to Italy. She remarks that an experience needs to sink into her mind as memory before she can write a poem about it, which reminds me of the English Lake District daffodils that "flashed upon" Wordsworth's "inward eye" in his poem "I Wandered Lonely as a Cloud." Which reminds me of the daffodils I myself saw on a springtime trip to the Lake District years before.

Meanwhile, still on the topic of Classical Greek literature, Marie-Claire brings up the philosopher-poet Lucretius, whose *De rerum natura* strongly influenced her. She says his assertion that nothing exists beyond physical matter gave rise to her own thinking, "that I am a system of atoms which formed itself like many other systems, and which has a slower entropy than most other systems of atoms. I don't believe in the infinite. I think earthly things are destined to die like the earth itself. And this common death brings us much closer to the animals, plants, and all things on Earth. I don't think there's any fundamental difference between us and these other things; for example, between my cat and myself."

Argos squinches his eyes. He begs to differ.

Sans dresser d'ombre

Le chat tout entier dans ses yeux
est la pensée d'un chat
qui se félicite, au milieu de sa figure triangulaire,
de ne pas être cet homme
si proche de lui
qui dort aveugle, sans dresser d'ombre sous la lune

et le matin
voit des choses
plates
comme ses pas

incapable de sauter sur les meubles
pour dominer la grisaille du jour.

Without Casting a Shadow

In its own eyes, the whole cat
is the thought of a cat
pleased, in the middle of its triangular face,
to not be this
nearby man
who sleeps blind, casts no shadow under the moon

and come morning
sees things
flat
like his feet

unable to pounce on the furniture
to tower over the dullness of the day.

A SPARROW ALIGHTS on the windowsill, rousing Argos up on his haunches. His eyes are bright and focused. He pounces onto the plant stand by the window, somehow managing to not topple the roses. His uber-feline coordination, plus Marie-Claire's inattention to his movements, tells me he's done this many times before.

"So, no fundamental difference between plants, animals, and us. Between you and Argos," I say, holding my hand out, inviting him to at least sniff it. He literally bats it away.

"I'm not saying he's humanlike," Marie-Claire says.

"I'm beginning to think he might be," I say.

"I'm not an anthropomorphist," she continues with a laugh, "but I believe we are made of the same fundamental material, the atoms in Argos no different than the atoms in you or me."

This compelling clarity of her worldview, combined with her signature spareness and precise word choices, enable her poems to express the physical unity we humans share with the natural world—while resolutely resisting any anthropomorphic reading. A close reading of her sister poems "Embolism" and "...In You" offer insight into the way this works.

Embolie

Une goutte d'air
dans un canal de sève
fatigué de boire à la terre :

l'embolie s'empare
de l'arbre entier

il meurt

se renferme
dans sa mémoire.

Longtemps d'apparence intouché
brusquement
il s'abat
sous le poids d'un oiseau

devient moignon ...

Embolism

A drop of air
in a sap canal
tired of drinking from earth:

the embolism seizes
the whole tree

dies

retreats
into its memory.

Looks untouched for a long time
suddenly
collapses
under the weight of a bird

becomes stump ...

. . . En toi

L'ombre du moignon d'orme sur rivière
entre dans tes yeux
descend
à l'intérieur du corps

se met en place au lieu
de la tumeur qu'on a coupée extraite
voici bien des années, sans savoir
qu'on préparait logis au reflet d'arbre mutilé

maintenant, que faire
de cette irruption
vigoureuse
en toi ?

. . . In You

The elm stump's shadow on river
enters your eyes
descends
to the body's interior

takes the place
of the tumor they took out
years ago without knowing
they'd readied a home for the maimed tree's reflection

now, what to do
with this vital
burst
inside you?

IN "EMBOLISM," a tree with apparent humanlike volition is "tired of drinking from earth" and has an embolism. It then dies and "retreats into its memory," where it becomes a shadow of itself. The shadow ". . . In You" enters the onlooker's passive body and merges with the cavity left behind after a tumor's removal. Tree and person are joined in the mutual death of their cells: the atoms that once constituted the tree trunk and the tumor have dispersed into other systems. Perhaps they are now riverbed mud. Perhaps a willow or hollow reed.

Over the ten years preceding the interview, my mother had had several tumors removed from her body. Although I wasn't brave enough to visualize the resulting cavities in her body merging with the shadow memory of a tree, Marie-Claire's idea of this intimate mutuality with nature struck me as strangely comforting. My mother passed away a year and a half after my trip to Paris; by that time, the idea had grown into a wild garden on which I could graft the heartache of her illness and death. Over the subsequent ten years, I sowed a book of poems that helped me process her death and my grief. Thanks to paths of thought grooved out by Marie-Claire, I was able to write poems that merged my mother with the flora and fauna that fleshed out the estuaries, rivers, beaches, and singular lake of the shoreline town where I grew up; where she'd grown up before me. It was the land my mother loved. Land that, decades after moving away, still feels like a physical part of me. I have a deep and abiding faith that it is.

The Faith I Had in Death

by C. Cook

Silt settled on shad in the silk-black riverbed mud.
One time, willows, the slow world of sound, and the rot
of a tide-abandoned eel. What tempered the oaks

was the same soundless chant: waves reduced to glass.
When I was a cloistered child, convening
with the half-set sun, I saw a single lapwing land

in a dogwood whose dead red limbs had spread
like veins above the sedge; or was that I jutting out
of the reeds; my body that stiffened and stayed there, hollow

as a dance the damp air did with circuitous strands
of light? What remained was feathers
and wind, wood and my fearless old habit

of failing to summon a silence that outlasted the faith
I had in death. When I was an autumn child led
by winter's feeble torchlight, I saw snow settle on the bird's white

breast without melting. I prayed, but my words
were the shells of turtles, and my way was the way
the lapwing always circled back to the stick.

WHEN MARIE-CLAIRE SHIFTS in her seat and says, "For me, writing must above all include concrete experience, whether real or imagined," my then-self takes special note of it—and my future self heartily agrees with the sentiment. Marie-Claire continues: "The experience could be, for example, about a huge expanse of sky or about tiny leaves in a tree, but it must be something concrete that strikes me. Writing poetry really comes from our hearts' and memories' reaction to something concrete."

She says that, although technology has changed dramatically over the course of these four decades, pen and paper are still critical to her writing process: "I still need my body to participate in the poem." Marie-Claire's very process of writing poetry enacts the intimate physical connection to the world which the language of her poetry expresses. Her poems reflect in minute detail the body's physical location in the world, grounded in her travels abroad or her beloved Paris. At the same time, she conveys the body's interior experience in equally minute detail, creating a silent internal-external dialogue for which the poem, ironically, is the vehicle. In this way, it is as if her poems live on the lip of a mirror, able to see the fully fleshed physicality, its reflection, and what is hidden within it, all at once.

Alain knocks on the door and opens it just enough to fit his head through. "Excusez-moi mesdames; Marie-Claire, ton médecin est au bout du fil, il t'appelle."

Marie-Claire excuses herself to take the call. I press my palms against the smooth wooden arm of the chair, feeling its grain and wondering how many poems she'd written here. I look across the room at her wall of books, watch them turn amber in the late morning light. My body commits all of this to memory: the sound of children playing in the courtyard outside; the aroma of coffee coming from the kitchen; the silky fur of Argos, who has finally let me pet him.

Chapter Three

Un langage du désir | A Language of Desire

MARIE-CLAIRE RETURNS to find Argos in my lap. She laughs and sits down, says that health issues stemming from her childhood illness continue to plague her, as they have her whole life. This is why a stimulating interior life has always been so important to her.

Establishing such a life in academics wasn't without its hurdles. When she was finally able to attend school after the war and her protracted hospitalization, she says, "I had to do an enormous amount of work to catch up to my peers. Although I excelled in some subjects, such as literature, there were others I didn't know at all. For example, I didn't know what a right angle was, or other very elementary things, because I'd had no schooling, none at all. But I promised myself never to worry, because I'd overcome that terrible experience, and because my studies genuinely interested me."

While Marie-Claire's passion for reading and research drew her to literary scholarship, her harrowing wartime illness catalyzed a need to write poetry. And when her education progressed to the point where she needed to choose a research subject for her thesis, she was very clear about keeping her scholarly writing and creative writing separate.

"I decided against researching contemporary poetry because I thought it would prevent me from writing my own kind of poetry," she says. "I thought the contagion would be too strong."

I think of the contagion that had spread from Wordsworth's poetry to mine; what a challenge it was to develop my own poetic voice when steeping myself in the study of his.

"So I chose to do my thesis on prose writing of the nineteenth century. It's an epoch in French literature that interested me because it had the same problems we had then and still have today: racism, war, drugs. And in choosing to focus on nineteenth-century prose, I didn't risk contagion."

Marie-Claire's decision not only created space for her to develop her own style of poetry, but also led her to become a renowned scholar on the literature of that era, particularly on the work of Anatole France. She edited the distinguished Pléiade multivolume edition of France's novels and short stories and went on to write several books about his work.

When it comes to literary criticism, she tells me she's especially interested in "philosophies that consider how poetry reveals the meaning of existence in the temporal world, such as in the works of Kierkegaard and Heidegger"; that she's averse to such schools of criticism as "the linguistic theory that predominated French critical thought from the 1960s through the 1980s [which] is extremely weak in its ability to explain poetry. Its vocabulary creates a closed circle: when you read linguistic theory, you return to language as a mode of communicating with one another. However, poetry is not a language of communication. It is an exception in language, because each poet has their own language.

"Academic writing teaches students how to be better critical thinkers, better readers of poetry, and also to better understand certain things about the world and the people in it," she continues, "but the deeply profound things about the world and people—these can only be learned from poetry itself."

Marie-Claire goes on to say that while choosing not to study contemporary poetry enabled her to develop her own unique style, there were three contemporary poets who did influence her when she first started writing poetry seriously in the early 1950s:

"Yves Bonnefoy told me to have confidence in my poetry and to pursue my poetry like I was pursuing hope. And then André Frénaud. He is, well, violence. He is a poet who writes in a scathing language of liberty. Henri Michaux is the poet who's had perhaps the greatest influence on me in terms of my sensibilities. He is a poet of the heart, of the unhappiness of the heart, and even died of a heart attack. He withstood much in his life and felt the need to release his burdens in his writing. This really struck me."

I remark that all these poets are men.

"I don't think that there is a writing particular to women," Marie-Claire responds. "What I do really doesn't differ radically from what my male poet friends do, in the sense that human nature, common to all of us, is what lies at the heart of our poetry. A poem isn't marked by a masculine or feminine voice or style. There is nothing specifically feminine about my poetry. But in one particular poem, I did choose to speak in a distinctly female voice."

She pulls a copy of *Mémoire d'abolie* out of her bookshelf and thumbs through it until she finds the poem she's looking for.

Femme

Je superpose
Je renâcle
J'attise au discours de l'homme

Je détourne
J'absente
Je croise un visage buté

Je suis tout ce qui grouille en pelletée de terre
Contre-immuable
Sillonné d'insomnies

Je lui passe mon temps
Ses mots sont arrachés.

Woman

I superimpose
I speak out
I stir up man's discourse

I divert
I vacate
I cross a stubborn face

I'm all that swarms in shovelfuls of earth
Against entrenchment
Furrowed with insomnia

I give him my time
His words weeded out

"THIS POEM LOOKS at rhetorical male discourse, a discourse in decline, an inflexible discourse which is not that of poetry. But I understand masculine discourse, because to undertake my studies and to be a university professor, naturally, you have to participate in it. Consequently, I use this discourse in writing books of literary criticism, but it's not the only possible discourse for discussing poetry critically. I also seek alternative discourses."

Marie-Claire notes, too, that rhetorical male discourse is what created gender inequality.

"For a long time, it was actually written in the French Constitution that women were not the equals of men. I had firsthand knowledge of this legal inequality. For example, the first time I wanted to open a bank account, I had all the necessary documents with me and I had money to deposit, of course, but when I got to the bank, they told me I was missing one thing: my husband's written permission. I had a job, just as he did. I earned money, just as he did, but I could not open a bank account without my husband's consent."

I shake my head but am not shocked. "Women's rights have come a long way since then, in some regards," I say. "In other regards, not so much."

"*C'est vrai*, a masculine mentality remains even today. More equitable laws have only gotten us so far. Social obstacles remain, such as a certain reigning idea of 'femininity,' which begins with the education of the little girl: grooming her more passive, more dependent, more 'suitable' qualities. But to be a creator, one must dare to bring the dark depths of the inner well out into the light, and try to exercise control of it.

"It is a kind of seizure of power, transgression, which is not always acceptable for women to do, especially in France. Because what comes up from the bottom of the well is desire, eros. This has long been restricted, even taboo, for women. And those who restrain a woman's desire restrain not only her sexuality but also her artistic joys: poets who just pour their words into a ready-made mold have little chance of writing a good poem. Paradoxical, perhaps, that the only place where the taboo of eros was lifted for a woman, in centuries past, was the convent, where their love had the right to rush toward God. And what sensuality, what a language of desire among mystical women!"

Été

Tous feux éteints, l'été
prend règne sur thyms et lavandes
avec un goût d'essences pures, rond en bouche
qui descend
vers le centre du corps
chaleureux jusqu'au sexe.

On aspire les causses
en fièvre de plaisir.

Summer

All fires snuffed, summer
rules sovereign over thyme and lavender
a taste of their essence, plump in the mouth,
descends
to the body's core
warm down to the sex.

We inhale the karst's gorges, rivers, and caverns
in fevered pleasure.

WHEN TRANSLATING "SUMMER," I made a decision that I rarely make as a translator: to replace a word (*"les causses,"* which strictly translates to "the causses") with more descriptive language ("the karst's gorges, rivers, and caves"). In Marie-Claire's original, *"les causses"* refers to a region of southwestern France known for its dramatic and otherworldly landscape: porous limestone plateaus riven with gorges and hidden grottoes; river-carved canyons and surreal rock formations. For most French readers, *"les causses"* evokes a clear image of this landscape, but "the Causses," "the karst," or even "the limestone plateau" would evoke no such image for most readers of the English translation. My goal in translating the word was to more closely replicate not the original text, but rather the sensual impression that text made on the source-language reader.

The fact that cave paintings in the Causses have yielded evidence of prehistoric man further enriches the poem's meaning for many French readers, especially as it taps into themes that run through Marie-Claire's work. I tried to work this meaning into the line as well, but as much as this added information may have enlightened the reader, it overburdened the line and departed too far from the original text. I leave it to the reader, then, to infer the prehistoric possibilities in such a landscape.

In terms of "a language of desire," this poem certainly matches any female mystic's expression of an erotic sacred union with the divine—except there is no divinity, no transcendence, nothing beyond the intimate physical experience of uniting with one's natural surroundings. After translating this poem in 2008, I reread Marie-Claire's definition of the sacred in her introduction to *Rituel d'emportement*:

La mort peut être un solide point d'appui, une évidence dans le déchirement, qui éclaire la terre et fait estimer la vie, sentir que les rencontres avec les gens et les choses sont précieuses, uniques. Une évidence, aussi, pour amener à considérer qu'il existe un sacré : non pas par rapport à une religion révélée, mais par rapport à l'ensemble des choses — disons au cosmos, dont le grande mouvement, à la vie, à la mort, à la vie de nouveau, est une respiration concrète qui nous englobe tous.[6]

✳ ✳ ✳

Death can be a solid point of support, evidence in the wrenching apart that illuminates the earth and makes us value life; makes us feel that encounters with people and things are precious, unique. Evidence, too, that leads us to consider a sacredness: not in relation to a revealed religion, but in relation to all things— let's say to the cosmos, whose great movement, to life, to death, to life again, is a concrete breathing that encompasses us all.

After rereading it, I emailed Marie-Claire, asking if she could expand on her idea of "the sacred." She responded: "For me, 'the sacred' refers, without any meaning of transcendence, to the sense of that which is at the origins of nature and life, and which appears to us in its force, without our being able to explain it. But the poet feels it and tries to express it, with words that neither refer to divinities nor philosophical concepts."

At the time, I was struggling to come to terms with the extent to which the Church had failed women in my family for generations, extending all the way back to our Irish roots—had castigated them for premarital sex, excommunicated them for divorcing, administered last rites with a cold lack of compassion; the list goes on. In the throes of this struggle to fill the spiritual sinkhole it had created in my life, I found in Marie-Claire's poem "Summer" a deeply satisfying simplicity, purity, and wholeness. Beyond the proverbial "breath of fresh air," the inhalation of "the karst's gorges, rivers, and caverns" felt earthy, feminine; far from the patriarchal institution whose sovereign divinity and philosophical concepts, proscribed by the rhetorical male discourse, had restricted the flow of my spirituality, sexuality, and creativity over the course of my whole life. It was a dam-break that Wordsworth's pantheistic notions of immortality had never released in me.

Solstice

by C. Cook

Prologued to the point
                of nonexistence,

the longest day leans
        into the moon-moist loins of night.

Seas drained by sun-long tongues
        of light now speak the language of sweat

and dew: midnight's mirrored beads
            weigh dawn's pockets down

like the bones of a cave bear
        whose flesh still fructifies the soil.

Begonias bloom froth-blue above
        their scalloped leaves.

Lilies lift their mouths moonward, lips brimming
                    with
                      droplets:
moments before, they were no more
than a moist remembering.

Once praised by the blaze of an average-sized star,
Earth tips her body back to a blackness

that's been barren without her.

Chapter Four

Un orangé dans la confiture | A Solar Hue in the Marmalade

WHEN OUR INTERVIEW ENDS, Marie-Claire signs a copy of her latest book of poetry, *Avec la mort, quartier d'orange entre les dents*, and gives it to me. Then she invites me to stay for lunch, an invitation that I am delighted to accept. After ushering me into their living room with a glass of lemonade, she joins Alain in the kitchen to prepare the midday meal. I sit on their cream-colored jacquard sofa and place the books she gave me on the coffee table beside a Gallé art glass vase. The room is decorated with turn-of-the-century antiques in the Art Nouveau style. A four-panel painted silk screen—such as one might imagine positioned between a one-armed fainting couch and a vanity table in the lady's bedroom of a Balzac novel—hangs on one wall.

I place my glass beside the Gallé vase and think back to a trip I took in 1984 with my grandmother, an avid collector of Art Nouveau glass. We drove to the Corning Museum of Glass in upstate New York to see an exhibit titled "Emile Gallé: Dreams into Glass." I still have the exhibit catalog, a beautiful book in its own right, which my grandmother bought for me. Gallé art glass has an ethereal quality, as if its exquisite beauty exists in a vacuum of purity and serenity. It's a quality I connect with the "angel of the house" trope in turn-of-the-century Europe, where men's grubby Industrial-Age work (physically or ethically grubby, depending on their social class) necessitated having a domestic "angel" to come home to. This cultural imperative required perfect purity on the part of wives and women to bring the whole system into balance.

If Marie-Claire's living room was a testament to exquisite pieces of art, her poetry is a testament to their shadow side. Just as every atom's positron has its antimatter twin in an electron, every Gallé vase has its point-of-shooter video game and battle tank (indeed, when German tanks started rolling through Paris in World War I, Gallé's widow shut down her late husband's glassworks).

Farces et attrapes

Les façades début de siècle (celui d'avant)
n'ont pas achevé d'engloutir
le tagliatelles qui sculptent en désordre
fenêtres et portes.
Au milieu de la rue
avance un tank dernier modèle.
Derrière un rideau l'enfant
assis à sa console de jeux
tente d'anéantir au rayon de la mort
un groupe en fuite, aux enjambées pas souples,
exode d'hommes virtuels.

— Combien de temps, ah combien de temps
va rester cette scène en l'état ?
demandent sous le macadam
les morts mérovingiens mêlés aux caillasses.

Ils approchent de la surface
quand elle éclate, confondant
l'ancien et le nouveau, leur poussière, les rêves de Gallé,
les chairs de l'enfant, des soldats.

Seul est resté intact à quelques mètres
un magasin de farces et attrapes
dont le gérant remercie Dieu.

Joke

The turn of the last century's facades
haven't finished devouring
the tagliatelles that mangle
windows and doors.
Down the middle of the street
advances a late-model tank.
Behind a curtain the child
at his game console
tries to destroy by death ray
a group of limping fugitives,
exodus of virtual men.

—How long, ah how long
will the scene remain thus?
ask, from under the tarmac,
the dead Merovingians mixed in with the stones.

They surge to the surface
when the scene explodes, mingling
ashes of lives ancient and new with the dreams of Gallé,
flesh of the child with flesh of the soldiers.

The only intact thing, some meters down,
is a joke shop
whose manager thanks God.

THE MEROVINGIANS, seen here literally turning in their graves, hail from the Frankish dynasty that established the modern nation of France in the sixth to eighth centuries. The dynasty's mythical origin story includes ancient Greek themes (their founder was conceived when a sea beast known as the Quinotaur raped his mother) as well as Christian ones (the child of Mary Magdalene and Jesus Christ married into the French royal line, engendering the quasi-divine dynasty). So "when the scene explodes," Merovingian bodies "surge to the surface" with fossilized stones and shells from the bed of the Paris Basin, which cradled a part of the Paleogene North Sea one hundred million years before.

Mer ancienne

Bruyères
à l'automne des montagnes

au printemps, c'est de nouveau leur étendue mauve.

Toison caressable toute l'année, comme celle d'un ventre.

Sol sourd aux pas, on avance, s'agenouille, rafraîchit sa joue,
on voudrait que toutes les fleurs se distillent en liqueur qu'on
boirait, magique,
descendant jusqu'à des coquillages enfouis,

une mer ancienne,
sur laquelle on dériverait, bouche sur le sein caché depuis des
millénaires.

Ancient Sea

Clusters of heather
in the autumn mountains

spring, and they're once again a mauve expanse.

A year of caressable fleece, like an underbelly.

Turf deaf to footsteps, we go along, kneel, cool our cheek,
we'd like the flowers to distill themselves into liquor for us
to drink, magic,
down to the buried shells,

an ancient sea
on which we'd drift, mouth to breast hidden for
millennia.

IN THE CORNER of the living room, a curio cabinet holds a large collection of geodes, shells, petrified wood, mineralogical specimens, and what looks to be the fossil of a prehistoric fish. I'm just about to walk over for a closer look, when Argos jumps onto the sofa arm and pads across the cushions into my lap. Not wanting to betray what I take to be his budding trust in me, I satisfy myself by looking at Marie-Claire's cabinet of curiosities from afar.

Depuis

Les va-et-vient de l'univers prennent toutes leurs aises.

Depuis le fossile et sa gangue minérale, une généalogie se déroule, évidente,
coquillage, poisson, poumons très doucement issus des branchies,
sauriens à pattes courtes,
jusqu'à notre chatte aux yeux bleus.

Et nous : l'hésitation entre eux et une race dont nous n'avons pas idée ? Retournant peut-être vers une haute mer ?

From

The comings and goings of the universe take their time.

From the fossil and its host rock, a genealogy
unfolds, self-evident,
shells, fish, lungs emerge gently from gills,
short-legged reptiles,
all the way to our blue-eyed cat.

And us: the pause between all this and an as-yet unknown race?
Returning, perhaps, to a higher sea?

MARIE-CLAIRE COMES IN to tell me lunch is ready, but blue-eyed Argos won't budge from my lap. She laughs and claps her hands brusquely in his direction. He hops down and sniffs the ball-and-claw feet of the curio cabinet, as if he were going to do that anyway.

I take my seat in the Bancquarts' elegant dining room. Three wide-open French windows invite a warm breeze into the room, rustling the drapes and drawing my attention to their view of the Eiffel Tower. Alain pours a jewel-colored Beaujolais into small Moroccan glasses set before us. Marie-Claire brings out a series of small courses, first a slice of cantaloupe drizzled with port wine, then torn pieces of a crusty baguette, followed by cold slices of beef served with Dijon mustard and sautéed haricots verts, then a simple salad of lettuce and sliced tomatoes lightly tossed with olive oil.

The tomatoes taste particularly fresh, particularly flavorful. They bring to mind an alpine meadow in Kobarid, Slovenia, through which I walked the week before. It was the site of a World War I battle that decimated Italian troops, many of whom died with tomatoes from home in their pockets. These tomatoes sank with soldiers' flesh into the soil and self-seeded, transforming the battlefield into a meadow alive with wild Roma tomatoes every summer since.

As I chew the tomato's tender red flesh, my unsettling memory merges with Marie-Claire's views about the symbiotic exchange of flesh and blood between people and plants; her idea that death is the ultimate manifestation of this symbiosis. As I swallow the jellied seeds, an amorphous thought-form collects from the corners of my mind. This thought-form would go on to haunt me for years, like a dream that does no more than dip its toe into my consciousness. But, over time, my persistent efforts to coax it out onto the page eventually succeeded.

Tomatoes of Kobarid

by C. Cook

The tomato his bride planted like a kiss
in his breast pocket
                              beat
against his ribs as he marched
among fellow soldiers,
each with the heart
of his own wife's garden
                                        beating
against his own cage of ribs.

A whole troop of Roma
tomatoes too precious to cede to teeth
and tongue
                      marched to an alpine meadow
sweet with the lingering hum of summer
insects, soft
with the stamens of lacy white edelweiss.

What opened fire then was not the sun
blazing above Mount Triglav
nor the Carniolan lilies
                                    erupting
into orange bloom.

              No, what opened
fire opened
men's ribs to the soil.
Red flesh
and seeds' sweet jelly spurted through riven skin,
soaked wool tunics,

crimsoned boot-black soles,
sunk into bodies and blades
of grass,
        root-deep, stone-deep, bone-deep dirt
now yields a field of wild
Roma tomatoes summer
after summer.

SOMETIMES A POEM releases the thought-form that fathered it like a sliver tweezed out of flesh. But sometimes the flesh holds onto it, as mine held onto this one. Years later, I was still trying to tweeze it out, this time while writing a novel that features an alchemist living in seventeenth-century Philadelphia:

Kelpius forked a slice of tomato onto his earthenware plate. He harbored little hope that the New-World soil would produce food with the least bit of flavor or nourishment, since it was not yet primed—not like his family's Transylvanian farmland, where carrots, turnips, beets, and potatoes grew up through gruesome relics of ancient wars waged by voivodes Vlad Dracule and Vlad the Impaler. His grandmother said these relics, together with the blood-enriched soil that harbored them, gave the vegetables a nutty flavor rivaling the taste of any meat.

"Ces tomates sont délicieuses," I say.
Marie-Claire says they buy all their produce from the market next door.
"Le marchand ne vend que les légumes les plus frais," adds Alain.
After our salad, Marie-Claire brings out an assortment of French cheeses, followed by orange marmalade pastries and chocolate-filled figs, all of which they brought back from a recent trip to Provence.

En échange

Le fruit mûr

son orangé
dans la confiture

doux-acide
sur une langue de décembre.

D'une épaisseur tendre de baume
Il délecte notre gorge.

In Return

The ripe fruit

its solar hue
in the marmalade

sweet-sour
on a December tongue.

A balsam-soft salve
That delights our throat.

Dans la bouche

Fourrant une figue de chocolat
on met double douceur dans sa bouche

— Un corps et la pluie tiède
interfèrent au jardin du Midi, où des fruits se détachent
pour s'écraser en roseur miellée sur un banc.

— Bien plus au Sud, voici l'Océan, crénelé de tours portugaises.

Deux époques de vie

deux continents

sur la langue.

In the Mouth

Chewing a chocolate-filled fig
you savor double sweetness

—A body and the tepid rain
intrude on a garden in the South of France, where fruit falls
to squish honey-pink on a bench.

—Far further South, the Ocean, crenellated with Portuguese towers.

Two life-epochs

two continents

on the tongue.

WHILE ALAIN CLEARS the dishes, Marie-Claire says they'd like to show me their favorite places in Paris, places largely less trodden by tourists. I respond with gratitude and enthusiasm, delighted that, rather than spending the rest of the day riding an open-topped sightseeing bus or perhaps just reading in a café, I was going to see Paris through Marie-Claire's Ulyssean lens. I begin to imagine us mining hidden histories; stepping into myth-shrouded spaces; crossing paths with a genealogy that unfolded from gills to the Gauls, from theropods to Visigoths, Burgundians, and Carolingians; from the Merovingian kings, who claimed to be descendants of Mary Magdalene and Jesus; from these ancient races all the way to—

Argos pads up to me and meows, interrupting the meandering thoughts in which I'd lost myself. He fixes his blue eyes on me.

"Argos vous aime bien," Marie-Claire says.

I smile and reach down to pet him, but he runs away. Again.

Chapter Five

Oui, l'intervalle | Yes, the Interval

BEFORE WE LEAVE, Alain shows me into his study. Two violins, a digital piano, and a bank of shelves bursting with books, albums, CDs, and cassettes line the room. It isn't messy, exactly, but bears the structured chaos of an extravagant mind, offering a rare glimpse at the workspace of one of Europe's leading composers of microtonal music. I look down the hallway into the workspace of France's most prolific poet, where I spent the morning. I consider the hallway: a narrow windowless space, an interval where the poetry of one and music of the other meet.

Along one wall of Alain's study is an elaborate computer and sound system on which Alain makes his microtonal magic. He sits down in front of the monitor and pulls up a chair for me, then opens a digital file from the piece he's currently composing. A second later, the computer screen morphs into a soundboard whose dizzying array of buttons, bars, and switches rivals the dashboard of a 747. He opens another file, this one featuring a vertical keyboard abutting a grid whose rows are more numerous and narrower than the neighboring keys.

"Let's hear a passage from *Livre du Labyrinthe*," he says, referring to the microtonal oratorio on which he and Marie-Claire collaborated. The piece was performed at Radio France's Salle Olivier Messiaen in 2000. Alain takes a CD recording of it from his bookshelf and gives it to me with a smile.

When he presses play, the individual tones become visible: they aren't coming from the black and white piano keys themselves, but rather from the gridded lines between them. Each of these lines, these intervals, expands to reveal a graphed field of even more tonal possibilities. It was as if Alain had reached into the quantum innards of music and found wavelengths of protosound to tease into existence. If Marie-Claire evokes the term *l'intervalle* to explore the mysterious gap between human consciousness and the natural world, Alain seeks to express its mysteries through music haunting and strange. A liminal feeling reverberates through my chest as we listen to the oratorio's second movement, "Mélodramme."

(Pasiphaé)
Ariane sort de sa boîte à coudre une pelote de fil noir.
Elle en dégage l'extrémité qui restera enroulée sur ses doigts.
Elle espère que la longueur de la pelote suffira
pour que Thésée aille jusqu'à son frère.
Elle ne sait pas que j'ai coupé la juste mesure
entre l'unique porte du dédale et mon fils Minotaure.

* * *

(Pasiphaë)
Ariadne takes a skein of black thread from her sewing box.
She unravels the end she'll keep coiled around her fingers.
She hopes it will be long enough
for Theseus to reach her brother.
She doesn't know I cut the exact length
from the maze's only door to my son the Minotaur.

Several months later, I would write a poem about my experience listening to the CD on a foggy predawn drive through Vermont to see my dying grandmother, Ingrid Nelson. She was ninety-four and had recently taken to calling me her best friend, having forgotten I was her granddaughter. She wasn't wrong, though—we loved to travel together, visit gardens and art museums and shop together, borrow each other's jewelry and scarves. All my life she'd taught me the language of living. Over the last few weeks, she'd begun to teach me the language of dying. The lessons were somatic rather than semantic: far-off looks and faint smiles, deep sighs that seemed to come out of nowhere. Cupping my youth-smooth cheek in her wrinkled hand. Nodding for reasons only her waning heart knew.

Driving Through Shrouds

by C. Cook

I drive through shrouds

of snow, listening
to a plucked violin;
sole stringed instrument
yearning for a bow.
                The colorless sky:
not gray
      not white, but wet
   and tangled in trees.

       Asphalt's black tongue bridges the gorge ahead.

I pass roadkill, unrecognizable
as animal, intestines uncoiled,
heart one lung and a paw
are all
      the scavengers left behind.
Smell of late fall fires,
a willow in the pyre
of its own fallen limbs.

        I cross another, higher, bridge.

The gaslight yellow
foliage of a birch, scarred
by a gray cocoon
spun from twigs, torn

leaves, dung:
                         inside,
half-caterpillar half-moth creatures
prepare for their weeklong lives.

                    I hear a familiar instrument

strangely played, horns
of moths ripping their birth-shroud.
                         Seed-borne white
silkfish spill
out the mouth of a milkweed husk,
drift across the highway, impossible
to discern from the snow.

                              So slow
is the wail of the mezzo-soprano,
so gradual the dawn of her grief,
                         it rises right where the white road pierces
          the cold horizon ahead.

MARIE-CLAIRE DRIFTS IN from the hallway, joins us. "Alain and I have worked on several collaborations together," she says. "We've developed a method of transferring the techniques of one art form into the other in such a way that two works combine to create an autonomous third work. Alain wrote an essay about our collaborative work in the book I gave you earlier."[7]

I'd go on to read the essay on my flight back home the next day. In it, Alain writes of their joint effort to create "a harmony whose suppleness, thanks to microintervals, is in intimate relation with the rhythm of the words." He describes their work as "a permanent exchange, not only of ideas, but of methods or means, an exchange of worldviews." It's clear that the profound understanding and deep respect they had for each other's work over the course of their individual careers and shared lives is what generated collaborations as powerful as *Livre du Labyrinthe.* To convey the critical importance that "intervals" play in their joint work, he quotes from Marie-Claire's poem "Interval," noting that "un fragment de seconde blanche est notre différence" (a fragment of a second half note is our difference).

Intervalle

(from Opéra des limites, *1988)*

Mes doigts aux empreintes uniques
cirent une empreinte d'aubier
avec la dévotion de Véronique enlevant
sur la face du Christ
sa propre souillure.

Quand le chat miaule, un son
cherche à exister seul
comme un chapiteau sans colonne.

Vêtue en femme, je sors
de même terre que cet arbre
dont les années
sont incluses en stries dans le meuble.

Un fragment de seconde blanche
est notre différence.

Un son en marge d'animal.

Il ne fait pas encore silence.

L'intervalle
est mince et capital.

Interval

My fingers with their unique imprints
wax a sapwood's imprint
with the devotion of Veronica removing
from Christ's face
his own defilement.

When the cat meows, a sound
seeks to exist alone
like a decorative column top
without the column.

Dressed as a woman, I go forth
from the same earth as this tree
whose years
are girdled into the furniture's grain.

A fragment of a second half note
is our difference.

A sound after animal

but before silence.

The interval
is gossamer and material.

I THINK OF THE LINES "A fragment of a second half note / is our difference. // A sound after animal / but before silence" while listening to *Livre du Labyrinthe*'s Pasiphaë sing about Theseus's transformation into the Minotaur (the half-man half-animal monster she conceived when lying with a white bull) in the oratorio's first movement, "Thésée."

> Regard du Minotaure : un miroir de très ancien sang,
> où les choses
> habitent fort, dans la dépossession des mots.
> Un silence de pierre
> et d'animal.
> Un dédale en dehors des minutes.

* * *

> Gaze of the Minotaur: a mirror of most ancient blood,
> where things
> live robustly, dispossessed of words.
> A silence of stone
> and animal.
> A maze outside minutes.

In the CD's liner notes, Alain describes this moment as a textual event where "the Minotaur belongs to both the human realm and animal realm," as well as a musical event "for the clarinet and cello that, previously opposing one another, gradually join together into a perfectly homophonic finale."

The Bancquarts' epic retelling of Theseus and the Minotaur, like all of Marie-Claire's myth-inspired poetry, could be read as the hero's struggle to overcome obstacles destined by deities with invariably fragile egos. Or it could be read as the ordinary person's struggle to reconcile the relentless duality and permanent impermanence of their very existence. Which struggle plays out just depends on what side of the mirror you're on.

Intervalle

(from Avec la mort, quartier d'orange entre les dents, *2005)*

Derrière le miroir on se verrait au juste

mais devant lui
toujours
devant
on ne se connaît pas tout à fait

on demeure avec soi
qui n'est pas
complètement soi

on s'engage en conversation
on interdit à soi de s'en aller
de peur de s'ennuyer tout seul
on met en route un mot
à distance.

L'intervalle a de ces délices.

Dans un miroir
on a de quoi unir et désunir
on se dit :
mes mots
peut-être
tiennent le fil de la combinaison et du hasard.

Interval

Behind the mirror you see yourself precisely

but in front of it
always
in front
you don't quite know who you are

you remain with the self
which is not
entirely your self

you engage in conversation
you forbid yourself to leave
for fear of being bored all alone
you launch a word
from a distance.

The interval has these charms.

A mirror enables you
to unite and divide
you tell yourself:
my words
perhaps
hold the thread of combination and chance.

Postmortem

by C. Cook

When the boundaries are erased, once again the wonder: that I exist.
—Dag Hammarskjöld

Not I, but the mangy cackle of gulls
and the reeds they beat flat when they land;

the garden whose gray-blue slate gave way to weeds
and bodies of voles deranged by death.

When my face is most in shadow, I find the moon
to be the dark epitome of itself:

soon to start over from zero,
becoming the answer I am

to the question, which I also am.
A light that waxes and wanes at once,

I am a trick of the witch: she who divides herself by two
is always one, in the end.

Wind whines through the hollow pipe
of night, softly, it is said

that she who halves her life by death will find herself
the twin of many such things.

Oui, l'intervalle

Tu crois te dépouiller
de l'intervalle ?

Tissé avec ton corps
tu n'en saurais tirer
nulle fibre
sans
filer toi-même comme un bas.

L'adhérence
elle est là, étrange :

tu ne fais qu'un avec l'écart mince, fondamental,
vers
le début d'abîme
et
le début de joie.

Yes, the Interval

You're thinking of stripping yourself
of the interval?

Woven in with your body
you wouldn't be able to uproot it
not a single fiber
without
running yourself like a stocking.

The adherence
is there, strange:

you're only one with the slight gap, inherent,
heading toward
the dawning abyss
and
the dawn of joy.

AFTER PLAYING a couple more movements from *Livre du Labyrinthe*, Alain closes the files and turns off the computer, morphing the screen back to blank-slate blackness. Marie-Claire asks if I'm ready to see Paris.

"Oui!" I say. I'm ready to see Marie-Claire's Paris, ready to explore the City of Light's reflections and mazes, its gardens, gazes, and liminal spaces, for myself.

Chapter Six

Paris plain-chant | Paris Plainsong

Tarot: VII. The Chariot

by C. Cook

The woman I see reflected

in the back window of the Bancquarts' car
as they steal me
into their secret City of Light
        is a blurry version of me.

I listen as Marie-Claire recounts a story of her city
too heartbreaking,
too hard to hear the whole of:

I was a child in the second world war.
memories of bombardments. very ill by the
sea, immobilized town where I was being treated
the bombardments began, we were evacuated
to Paris, but Paris was also being bombarded. I
remember the occupation, Every time I see the Place de la
Concorde, being there in a crowd of people
bombardments where I lived,
not very far from here.
the destruction two days afterward, I was eleven
not far from here. the odor
of the rotting corpses.
very disturbing memories.
then France war with the colonies Indochina
Algeria
possibly
third world war.
but A poet cannot live
in a paradise and have any relation to life:

the violence which exists in death
an idea about hope has followed me

With Death, a Segment of Orange

always leans toward a form of hope, a form of serenity, and you
apprehend this
only in the form of pain.
something that we cannot forget: the ugliness of reality.

I listen on as her words turn Paris
into portals
                    to earlier times and parallel people,
folding what is not of this world
into what is . . .

Paris plain-chant (extraits)

S'en aller ? Voir, seul, chez soi, un mince objet. Entrer. On se glisse
dans la ville d'habitation, le pain, le mica. Transgression majeure.

Femme,

dans la vitre d'un compartiment de métro, sous un
tunnel,
tu aperçois ton visage
pas bien précise

à la semblance
d'une photo tremblée, qu'on ne retiendra pas.

La voyageuse en face de toi raconte les origines de
sa maison construite en dix-neuf cents par son
bisaïeul,

s'interrompt, demande :
— « Savez-vous si les ongles des morts poussent
    longtemps ?
J'ai rêvé que ceux de son fils, mon grand-père,
avaient traversé le bois du cercueil »

Vous vous regardez avec gêne.

Vous avez touché à
ce qui n'est pas du monde.

Paris Plainsong[8] (excerpts)

*Slip away? To see, alone, at home, a gossamer object. To enter. Steal
into the city of dwelling, bread, mica. Major transgression.*

Woman,

in the window of a subterranean train car,

you see your face
imprecisely

like
a blurry photo we can't quite remember.

The traveler in front of you recounts the origins
of the house her great-grandfather built in 1900,

Interrupts herself, asks:
—"Do you know if the nails of the dead
     keep growing?
I dreamed that those of his son, my grandfather,
had crossed through the wood of his coffin"

You look at yourself with embarrassment.

You've touched
what is not of this world.

Voici le temps des pluies, des magazines
aux couvertures gondolées
qu'on achète au vol
pour lire dans l'autobus, vers la gare Saint-Lazare.

Impossible de les ouvrir
les manteaux humides se touchent.

Tu es requis par la bouche de la voisine
elle a dû rompre avec
un proche   la vie peut-être

elle s'est évertuée
a mis du rouge
sur ses lèvres-fissures

tu n'oses pas regarder ses yeux.

Dans l'odeur des laines mouillées
tu descends

sous l'abri, tu regardes le titre de couverture :
Nous avons perdu la musique.

Bonjour Rimbaud
c'est vrai
«*La musique savante manque à notre désir*»

Here comes the rain, magazines
with curled covers
that we buy on the fly
to read on the bus, toward Saint-Lazare Station.[9]

Unable to open them
wet coats touch.

Your seatmate demands your attention
she had to break away from
a loved one   life   perhaps

she tried hard
wore red
on her cracked lips

you don't dare look her in the eye.

Amidst the smell of wet wool
you descend

under shelter, you read the magazine cover:
We have lost music.

Yes, Rimbaud
It's true
"We cannot achieve the music and knowledge we crave"[10]

Tellement utile, Caïn. Pourquoi tuer
Abel, ce faux jeton, sauf
par impérieuse injonction divine ?

Tellement utile, Judas,
honoré par
d'aventureux dévots
comme jumeau du Christ.

Braconnages de révolte. Où, sinon
dans les plus étroites rues de Paris que brûle l'été ?
Elles débouchent sur une pauvre boulangerie juive
(pains azymes, gâteaux au cumin).

Station Saint-Paul, un kiosque expose
ses feuilles sur le tronc des arbres.
Titres : meurtre, violence, trahison,
sans que personne prenne garde à ces comptines.

Salut, père Caïn, père Judas
prolifiques
mais
votre aventure a descendu beaucoup d'étages.

Encore vaut-il mieux, seul, grommeler la mort
qui ne manquera pas sa planque, au bout de
                                    quelque rue,
dans le quartier où s'est pendu Nerval.

So useful, Cain. Why kill
Abel, that slug, save
by dire divine injunction?

So useful, Judas,
honored by
undaunted devotees
as Christ's twin.

Poaching other people's revolts. Otherwise
in the narrowest streets of Paris that burn in summertime
and open onto a poor Jewish bakery?[11]
(matzo, cumin cakes)

Saint-Paul Station,[12] a kiosk displays
Leaflets on tree trunks
proclaim *Murder, Violence, Betrayal*
No one reads these nursery rhymes.

Hail, Father Cain, Father Judas
prolific
but
your adventure has sunk many stories down.

Better yet to be alone, grumbling about Death,
who won't miss his hideout at the end of
                              some alley
in the neighborhood where Nerval hung himself.[13]

Chien de mendiant, chien de ministre ?
Il court sur le trottoir, laisse brisée.

Du plus haut au très bas il est

constellation au ciel
Sirius qui brille
en prodige majeur

mais fils de la Mort
qui garde les Enfers jusqu'à la descente de
                              Notre-Seigneur
une première fois venu
pour l'inviter aux noces de Cana du Louvre

(Véronèse l'a peint en gros plan, devant la nappe.)

Il accompagne aussi Nerval qui a parlé du Bal des
                                        Chiens
si mal famé
avant de terminer par sa nuit blanche et noire.

On tourne autour
du mot chien, de l'être chien,
sans parvenir au centre

chien décalé
comme cœur dans le corps.

Beggar's dog, minister's dog?
He runs down the sidewalk, leash broken.

From the highest to the lowest it is

a constellation in the sky
Sirius shines,
major marvel,

but Death's son

who guards the Underworld until the descent of
Our Lord
a first coming
to invite him to the wedding at Cana in the Louvre[14]

(Veronese painted this close-up, in front of the tablecloth.)

He also accompanies Nerval, who spoke of the notorious
Dog Ball[15]
before ceasing by way of his black and white night.[16]

We circle
the word *dog*, the being *dog*,
without reaching the center

Dog slightly askew
like a heart in the body.

Le matin se dédouble
pluvieux/ensoleillé
sur les arbres du rond-point Saint-Charles

parmi les reflets
tu te prévaux du droit d'épave
pour en ramasser un, très rouge,
et le jeter sur les façades.

Solitude fraise et fuchsia
solitude de sang
de sexes gonflés plein les chambres

chaud, furieux bain de jouvence !

Voici que
la ville entière
clapote rouge autour de toi.

Un autre jour, gris et mystérieux, sur le pont de Grenelle,

ah, tu sors tout entier de ta bouche

pour te confondre avec

ton haleine et la brume

qui voile à demi la Tour Eiffel. Tu te dissipes avec elles.

C'est bonheur.

The morning splits
rainy | sunny
the trees on the Saint Charles roundabout[17]

among the reflections
you avail yourself of the "right of wreck"[18]
to seize a crimson roadside scrap
and hurl it at the storefronts.

Solitude in strawberry and fuchsia
loneliness of blood
swollen sexes full rooms

hot, furious bath of youth!

Here
the whole city
splashes red around us.

Another day, mysterious and gray, on Pont de Grenelle,[19]

ah, your whole self comes out of your mouth

to mingle with

your breath and the mist

that half veils the Eiffel Tower.[20] Self, breath, mist dissipate

into happiness.

Hôpital Necker, dit «des Enfants malades».

Enfants, non, je ne vous aurai pas vanté
votre immobile vie envahie de poison.

Je ne vous aurai pas leurrés
en louant votre sacrifice :
l'os pour l'os de quel autre, les dents pour quelles
dents ?

Je ne vous aurai pas dit
comparez-vous
aux enfants tués par les bombes
aux enfants orphelins, aux enfants du sida.

Quand je vous regardais, je n'aimais plus les mots
ni ma ville.

Necker Hospital, called "The Sick Children's."[21]

Children, no, I wouldn't have immortalized you
your immobile life plundered by poison.

I wouldn't have lured you in
by glorifying the sacrifice
of your bones (for whose bones?), your teeth (for whose teeth?)

I wouldn't have told you
compare yourself
to children bombed
orphaned, infected with AIDS.

When I looked at you, I no longer liked words
nor my city.

Méconnue

Préhistorique, dure,
c'est notre Seine hier si bien élevée
qui répondait aux questions sur les nautes,
la place de Grève, les ponts.

Vols de mouettes
giroflées du vent.

Sauvage
toute en vagues
rivière qui charrie des arbres, des formes anonymes

Seine qui bat son temps de crue
hors du nôtre,

spirales, tourbillons,

qui parle une langue
sans cesse méconnue par nous,
commune avec
la forêt vierge et les plissements des montagnes.

Slighted

Prehistoric, rough,
it's our Seine only recently well-behaved
that answered questions about the Boatmen,[22]
the Place de Grève,[23] the bridges.

Gull-flight
wind's wallflowers.

Wild
wave-squalling
river that sweeps away trees, anonymous forms

Seine that thrashes above the flood stage
we set,

spiraling, swirling,

speaking a language
constantly dismissed by us,
common with
the virgin forest and fold mountains.[24]

Bien le bonjour

Tu te passes de toi tu
dis bien le bonjour à l'envers de ta peau
et même
à son endroit

tu suis le fleuve dans un vent à soixante-dix à l'heure
qui étourdit et turbine le corps
prend pouvoir sous les jupes
affole les oiseaux de mer drissés jusqu'ici

une sorte de port se dessine
entre les réservoirs, les tas de sable bâchés.

Toutes les mers dans la Seine.

Saccades, hourras, hoquets, leur matière
se déchaîne en étroites rives.

How Do You Do

You refrain from yourself
say *how do you do* to your skin's flip side
and even
to its up-side

you flow with the river in seventy-mile-an-hour winds
that daze and energize the body
power up under skirts
panic seabirds halyarded up to here

a sort of door appears
between the water tanks, the tarpaulined mounds of sand.

All seas inside the Seine.

Lurches, hurrahs, hiccups, their substance
breaks loose between narrow banks.

Chapter Seven

La parole des os | Bone-Speak

AFTER DRIVING us through "Plain-chant" portals all throughout Paris, Alain pulls into a streetside parking space. I swear it's no bigger than a phone booth, but our charioteer parks the car with ease. When he goes to turn off the ignition, Marie-Claire stays his hand so as to keep listening to the music.

"This is one of my favorite parts," she says, referring to *Livre du Labyrinthe*'s first movement, "Thésée."

Theseus's tenor voice wails through the car speakers, wracked with guilt for having killed so very many men. I can feel my arm hair stand on end. In words written by Marie-Claire, to the tune of Alain's microtones, he sings:

> Mon insomnie dénude des miroirs
> qu'habite soudain
> mon vrai visage : un caillot qui verse des pleurs.
>
> Je voudrais le quitter, me débarrasser de ma
> chair.

* * *

> My insomnia unveils mirrors
> in which my true face
> springs to life: a weeping clot.
>
> I'd like to leave it, rid myself of this flesh.

A motorcycle goes by, drowning out the rest of Theseus's agonizing revelation. When I can hear the music again, the narrator's bass voice is

relaying the scene in song: having exhumed his victims' corpses from
their communal grave, Theseus

> ouvre ses veines, fend ses os
> les offre à ses victimes.
> Mais aucun fantôme n'approche.
> Seul, plein d'amertume, Thésée
> lentement se joint à nouveau
> os après os, veines cousues aux veines

* * *

> opens his veins, splits his bones
> offers them to his victims.
> But not one ghost approaches.
> Alone, embittered, Theseus
> slowly stitches himself together again
> bone to bone, vein to vein

When Theseus's agonizing epiphany ends, Alain turns off the car. We discuss the music while walking down an alley that leads to a hidden arcade of antique shops. Though the summer sun is bright, not a single strand of light penetrates this narrow slip of alley. Some shops sell carpets so old that their country of origin has ceased to exist. Others feature furniture from the age of the Bourbon kings. Shopkeepers greet Marie-Claire and Alain with familiarity. Alain tells me that these shops—and probably some items in them—have been here for centuries.

We turn down an even narrower alley which, in turn, opens into a stone courtyard with a giant gnarled fig tree in the center. Its roots snake between the slates and wrap around random table legs. Lanterns are hung from its low limbs. Plump fruit bends its slender branches. The maître d' hurries over and kisses Alain and Marie-Claire on both cheeks. After a lighthearted exchange, Marie-Claire introduces me, then he leads us to their regular table, pulling out the chairs for Marie-Claire and for me. Soon after, a waiter brings out their favorite bottle of rosé and several appetizers to share. What follows is a sumptuous multicourse Lebanese meal accompanied by a bottle of old-vine Chablis, then coffee and dessert—all without any of us ordering a thing.

When we rise to leave, I wait for Marie-Claire and Alain to file out first, then I bring up the rear of our three-person troop. I notice that Marie-Claire's gait has become more stilted and slower over the course of the afternoon. I think back to something she told me in our morning interview—that writing the poem "My Bones" was an exercise in "imagin[ing] that I rid myself of my flesh and *just like that* I leave my flesh behind in a café. I go out with just my bones. I am very relieved, very light."

Mes os

Ils ont de beaux restes, mes os

déjà sciés c'est vrai
déjà
ravaudés
ils restent courageusement.
Ils tiennent
la chair, la peau, par-dessus eux.

Leur troupe, je l'emmène
et m'emmène avec elle
(vieille impression : ne pas *en être* tout à fait)
devant des vitrines de musées, section préhistoire
où, parmi des cailloux prétendument taillés, des flèches,
se montrent des fémurs à fractures visibles
mais recollées.

Comme quoi, dans dix mille et des ans,
mes chers os maintenant sur la macadam, vous pourrez figurer
dans des expositions montées après un labeur fou
près de canettes à bière et de mitraillettes,

tout ce fourbi qui
dans ma vie
m'aura fourbue.

My Bones

My bones have beautiful remains

already cut in two, it's true
already
reconnected
as they bravely remain,
holding
my flesh and skin on.

I take their troop along,
take myself along, too
(old notion: not really being *one of them*)
to museums' prehistory galleries
which exhibit, among supposedly carved stones and arrows,
femurs clearly broken
but reglued.

So, too, can you, dear bones here on the asphalt,
appear, some ten thousand years hence,
in exhibits mounted after maniacal toil
beside beer cans and machine guns,

this rack that
through my life
will have wracked me.

La parole des os

La parole des os
prend son ampleur.

Rien pour la retenir.

Nos mots-en-bouche sont détruits.

Les mots d'os
s'en vont doucement vers le noir :
enterrement du loup, mues de l'orvet, humus.

Dans la cendre commune
ils célèbrent le délice oblique des profanations.

Puis, nos squelettes reformés, ils viennent
vers les vivants, pour quelle annonce énigmatique ?

À force de battre la nuit
ont-ils outrepassé
la limite du négatif, dans un affleurement d'aurore ?

Bone-Speak

Bone-speak
spreads.

Nothing to hold it back.

Our words-in-mouth are destroyed,

where words of bones
go softly off to darkness:
the wolf's burial, the slowworm's sloughed-off tails, humus.

In the communal ash
they celebrate the profane with oblique delight.

Then, our retooled skeletons come
toward the living, for what enigmatic announcement?

Did their repeated defeat of the night
overstep
negativity's limits, in a flowering of dawn?

SEEING MARIE-CLAIRE'S pained movements, I start to understand the appeal of ridding oneself of one's flesh. But bones also make relentless demands on the body—especially her bones, which bear a permanent bent from her childhood illness. And then, of course, there's the matter of the organs, I think as I walk behind Marie-Claire and Alain, who are comparing our evening meal with the last time they dined there. I think of another thing she told me that morning:

> My poetry, and the poetry of many others, comes out of our hearts, out of the sounds we make, out of the physical movements of our writing. I am very attached to the idea that in our hearts we have things that are exposed, naked things that we cannot see. And we cannot predict which of these things will happen. Deep down, I find an enigma, a communion with the concrete things in the interior of my heart that may cause my death. Perhaps death will come to my heart, perhaps a bacterium in my heart, I don't know. Perhaps my heart is getting ready to beat no more, I don't know. But it is this enigma that brings me closer to the world . . . this Communion with the world that takes place in the heart.

Attifeur

S'y retrouver dans l'ordre
des poumons, du diaphragme
comme un insecte dans le cœur obscure d'une fleur ?

Ta bouche d'ombre
les archives de ton silence
tu essaies de les explorer

tu es cet absorbeur tremblant des mots
qui aimerait les attifer
en non-paroles
entrant direct dans la circulation du sang.

Embellisher

To find your way around in the order
of the lungs, the diaphragm
like an insect in the dark heart of a flower?

You try to explore
your shadow-mouth
the archives of your silence

you are this trembling absorber of words
which you want to embellish
with a wordlessness
that directly enters the bloodstream.

Terre

Épeler un mot murmuré par nos capillaires

suivre à la trace
le sang qui bat à notre poignet

aimer un gonflement des veines

participation
clandestine
à notre long voyage :

mis bout à bout
tous nos tuyaux à sang
font deux fois le tour de la terre.

Terre,
tes insectes, tes fleurs, tes divinités,
les as-tu disposés le long de ces routes ?

Earth

To spell a word whispered by our capillaries

to track
the blood pulsing through our wrist

to love a swell of the veins

clandestine
participation
in our long voyage:

placed end to end
our blood-pipes
circle the Earth's equator twice.

Earth,
did you arrange your insects, flowers, divinities
all along these routes?

I FEAR FOR MARIE-CLAIRE—then I feel her bravery and am immediately reminded of my mother's bravery. Back home, my mother knows exactly what's happening inside her body. I think back to my poetic re-imagining of the moment she saw the scans.

Ultrasound Noir

by C. Cook

When the doctor waved
her wand over your breast,
an ill-preserved noir film appeared

on the screen above,
detailing your inner sleek
Art Deco design.

She showed how your clean lines
and soaring arches morphed
into felon darkness,

and there, in the shadows
beneath your sleek sheath
hospital gown: she pointed to a lump

of sloth where chic should be,
rogue cells in the streamlined suites
of your body moderne.

TWO YEARS LATER, in the last month of her life, I would go on to write another poem in this vein, my mind trying to come to terms with what I imagined might be going on inside her body.

Cell Block
by C. Cook

I'm a girl born to a woman betrayed
by her basic unit of life.

Even now, my clock ticks backwards
while a vapor of bees spells

sweet in the bleak night sky.
I need no food she would have said

if she could speak
in her body's breatharian state.

I want no water, while malignancy
multiplied inside her like

her death depended on it: a mass
extinction of healthy cells,

and as for her bones,
they were shaped

like the skeleton key
to a lock later found in a distant

underground door. Inside
was a monastery of breathing, bees

building honeycomb cloisters one silent
hexagonal cell at a time.

Tarot

XV.

De face lui notre associé sans ombre
Mémoire sourde
Hors de sommeil
Mêlée dans nos tissus

Par toi sans nom
La voile va de mort en existence

Vers de grands feuilletages sur ton corps
Ver écailles d'ancêtres
Le monde gonfle

Et nous mal équipés pour le désir
Notre espace intérieur
Se lève
Se passe de nous

Il appareille
Pour ton immense lunaison.

Tarot

XV. The Devil

Facing our shadowless partner
Memory deaf
Deprived of sleep
Tissue-deep disturbance

Anonymous
Is the sail from death into existence

Toward a grand leafing over our body
Toward our ancestors' scales
The world swells

And we are ill-equipped for desire
Our interior space
Gets up
Goes on without us

Sets sail
For your immense moon.

Chapter Eight

L'intervalle habitable dans la réserve du dieu-lune |
The Livable Interval Left by the Moon

ON THE DRIVE back to my hotel, Alain plays the recording of another one of his and Marie-Claire's collaborations: "Suite au dieu-lune" was performed at Radio France in 1988 by A Sei Voci, a French vocal ensemble best known for their Renaissance and Baroque music. Their voices are full-bodied and oaky. The eerie yet strangely comforting microtonal harmonies bring to my drowsy mind the feeling of old-vine Chablis glowing honey-gold in my stomach. Eyes turned inward, I can almost watch the glow send viscous sleep to my organs, muscles, and mind, like lava through my nerves and meridians. As the car whisks us over the Pont de Grenelle, I look out the open window to see the moon: a pale yellow globe shimmering on the Seine.

Suite au dieu-lune (I–III)

I

Cendres sur la face
la lune étale au ciel les mystérieux suçons du destin
que nous sentons à notre peau
le soir
ayant déposé notre habit de souffles
pour être seuls dans une pièce à double rideaux.

Nous répétons alors
des gestes si anciens qu'ils sont hors de l'histoire
et marchent dans la chair de notre espèce
comme les bêtes près de nous
marchent dans les fibres des meubles.

Le temps échappe aux montres.
Sous elles
où bat visiblement le sang compulsé par le cœur
un doigt se pose.

Nous finissons toujours par écarter les étoffes.

Notre figure
un peu reflétée dans la vitre
dit allégeance aux millénaires.

II

Au crépuscule
se lève une incarnation de notre impalpable emblavure
                                                    au monde.

Abolie la distance entre nuage et nous.

L'intimité du sang avec la sève
se tisse à la lueur des meubles.

Notre corps la fleur et le dieu
tout est compact.

III

Dieu-lune
enveloppant de vent les hautes branches
attire un corps dans la rue verte du sommeil.

Des choses bougent
imperceptiblement et nous soulagent
d'être cette chair toute seule
qu'une force remue
par le dedans.

Une patte d'étrange
s'engage à travers les volets.

Shadowing the Moon-God (I–III)

I

Cinder face
moon scatters the sky with destiny's mysterious love bites
that nip our skin
at night
when we've cast off our cloak of breath
to be both of us alone in a two-curtained room.

Here we repeat gestures
older than history
that stride through our species' flesh
as beasts nearby
stride through the fibers of our furniture.

Time eludes watches
beneath which
blood, compelled by the heart, visibly pulses.
A finger rests.

We always finish by opening the drapes.

Our face
faintly reflected in the windowpane
pledges allegiance to the millennia.

II

Into twilight
rises an incarnation of our impalpably fertile world.

Eliminates the space between clouds and us.

Blood and sap blend: their intimacy
threads through the furniture's warm glow.

Our body the bloom and the god
all is close-grained.

III

Moon-god
wrapping high branches with a wind
which draws a body into the green street of sleep

Things move
imperceptibly and relieve us
of being this lone flesh
moved by a force
that comes from within.

An unfamiliar paw
comes through the shutters.

ALAIN TURNS THE CAR onto a cobblestone street, jarring me into a crescent of semiconsciousness. My eyes blink back to the morning interview, which now seems millennia rather than hours ago, when Marie-Claire explained her thinking as she wrote "Suite au dieu-lune." "Time eludes wristwatches," she said, because "the Cartesian manner by which we measure time has nothing to do with the interior time by which we live. And then, seeing 'our face faintly reflected in the windowpane' assures us that we are still alive, that another face hasn't replaced ours. Our face 'pledges allegiance to the millennia' because behind our face there are the faces of all the people who have lived before us and who may also have looked at their own reflections in a windowpane or a mirror."

The wind blows in from the car window, wrapping my face in its coolness and whipping a strand of hair loose from my bun. A light rain drizzles in. A Sei Voci's voices, Marie-Claire's words, and Alain's microtonal notes blend and buzz out the backseat speaker. I press my hand against it, feel it vibrate my flesh. An awareness of being at the mercy of the moon is the last conscious crumb I cling to before sleep steals even that from my mind. Before a Coltrane kind of smooth swing breeze blows by, high-brassed whines of a slow moody sax, lips girdling woodwind reeds, *Green Dolphin Street* slink as black & white & blue in mood as some low grove where Tarots jut from the moss: Star, Tower, Wheel of Fortune, luck in the dark of our jazz vespers, our life-laden houses of cards.

Suite au dieu-lune (IV–IX)

IV

Lune ?
Son visage est marqué par tumulte et pulsation fragile.

Elle participe au genre d'homme et de femme.

Nos yeux ouverts à l'intérieur de nous
sous les paupières endormies
suivent le cours de sa cueillaison :
langue gorge
et notre petite mœlle de vertébré.

Nos yeux ouverts épient sur le trajet des nerfs.

V

Notre vie proche d'autres vies
notre idée que l'amour est de la partie ?

C'est en fragments si minces dans les livres
les courses les bonjours les jardins le sommeil
qu'il faut assurer : j'aime
pour se persuader que l'ombre malheureuse
ne nous mange pas tout entiers
nous qui mangeons
des bêtes apprêtées sans yeux ni poils
pour ne pas voir le meurtre encastré dans l'amour.

Une lumière au ciel
c'est un astre mort depuis mille siècles.

Nous aussi sur d'autres planètes
nous sommes morts.

Amours délices de repas
c'étaient nos rayons en survie
pour des regards inattentifs et rares.

VI

Une interférence du vent
rafraîchit la lune près de ce visage étranger naguère,
maintenant proche pathétiquement,
jamais tien,
baisé en rêve.

Jamais confondu, jamais plus hors de toi.

Un glaçon dans les flammes.

Vent et visage
à peine possédés
présents à la fenêtre fraîche.

La nuit fait semblant de mourir.

C'est toujours
la longue intimité d'anis dans ta chair passagère.

VII

Les chers défunts prennent subitement connaissance
de leur beauté.
Ce lambeau très lent, brume sur lune, leur est affecté
pour se vêtir d'un sang plus spacieux que naguère.
Ils enveloppent le coudrier, l'iris, l'indigence diurne
des vivants. La terre tourne sa peau. Les chiens ne font plus
peur à ces aveugles en nous qui rejoignent chaque nuit la musique.

VIII

Nous avons avalé ton marais d'ombre
comme à travers la gorge des grands maudits
la couleuvre se faufile vers un ciel brûlé.

Le noir n'est pas absolu cependant.

Tu avances avec la lueur d'ardoise
dont brillent les monnaies dans les anciens tableaux.

Tu annonces le trottoir d'adieu momentané
quand il a plu sous les fenêtres et que ton œil
au bord du square évoque la mer.

IX

Il est des yeux pour qui les cerises ne sont jamais
                                                    mûres

des yeux qui ne voient pas le vert
qui vivent d'éternel automne.

Pourtant l'imperfection se tisse
d'une douceur qui va de mer au ciel.

Très rares
les aveugles au bleu.

Comme si flux reflux
laissaient intervalle habitable
dans la réserve du dieu-lune.

Shadowing the Moon-God (IV–IX)

IV

Moon?
Its face bears traces of frenzy and trembling.

It participates in the gender of man and woman.

Our open eyes turn inward
under their sleeping lids,
track the course of moon's harvest:
tongue throat
and the marrow encased by our vertebrae.

Our open eyes spy on the coursing of the nerves.

V

Our life close to other lives
our idea that love is essential?

It's in fragments so slender in books
errands hellos gardens sleep
that we néed assurance: I love
in order to convince myself that the despondent shadow
does not eat us whole
we who eat
beasts dressed minus eyes or hair
so we don't see the murder built into love.

A light in the sky
is a star dead for thousands of centuries.

We too, on other planets
are dead.

Loves mealtime delights
our rays reaching
for glances dreamy and rare.

VI

An interference of wind
freshens the moon near this face, so recently foreign
now woefully close,
never your own,
caressed in dream.

Never confused, never again outside of you.

A block of ice in the flames.

Wind and face,
scarcely possessed
frost the window.

The night pretends to die.

It's always
the enduring intimacy of anise in your fleeting flesh.

VII

The dearly departed take sudden note of their beauty.
This slow tatter, mist on moon, cloaks them in a blood more
spacious than before.
They wrap the hazel, the iris, the diurnal destitution
of the living. The earth turns its skin. The dogs no longer terrify
the sightless within us who merge each night with the music.

VIII

We've swallowed your dark swamp
as though through the throat of the damned
the grass snake sneaks toward a scorched sky.

The dark is not absolute, however.

With sheen you proceed along the slate
whose coins shine on in ancient paintings.

You announce the sidewalk of the brief goodbye
when rain has come in through the windows and your eye
at the edge of the public garden evokes the sea.

IX

There are eyes for which the cherries never ripen,

green-blind eyes
that live in eternal autumn.

Yet imperfection is woven
from a sweetness that threads through sea and sky.

Very rare
those blind to the blue.

As if ebb and flow
left a livable interval
in the moon-god's reserve.

Tarot

XXII.

Ce n'était pas fini
La terre

Elle a bien su
Nous relancer sur le hasard
D'une poussée à peine inexorable

Plénitude nourrie d'émeute
notre rencontre
connut l'imperfection

Au terme de sa vie c'est toujours le joueur apatride
Échiné au gémissement des arbres
Vivant son ventre avec difficulté

Une forteresse abandonnée
passa la ligne
d'un autre mur
s'identifia
tomba disloquée dans le temps

À quoi sers-tu creusé ?
— J'ai gravi le zéro du monde
Métamorphose est mon habit

J'ai cessé de brûler

Mon corps
a trouvé l'introuvable

Tel était le mot du silence, l'enjeu
De ce jeu tout entier dirigé vers la perte

Je marche
Vers la transhumance définitive

Rien ne me reste des mesures de la vie
Sinon
Ce grand voyage incompréhensible.

Tarot

XXII. The Fool

It wasn't finished
Earth

She well knew
To revive us on the chance
Of a barely inescapable push

Fullness fed by upheaval
our encounter knew imperfection

At the end of his life he's always the stateless player
Spine against the groaning of trees
Living his stomach with difficulty

An abandoned fortress
crossed the line
of another wall
identified itself
fell dislocated in time

What purpose does your hollow self serve?
— I climbed the world's great nothing
Dressed in metamorphosis

I stopped burning

My body
found the unfindable

Such was the word of silence, the point
Of this game always going toward loss

I walk
Toward conclusive transhumance

None of life's measures remain for me
Otherwise
This great incomprehensible journey.

Epilogue

Nos paupières s'ouvrent | Our Eyelids Open

MOON-GOD HAS EBBED and flowed endlessly since the drizzly night I bid the Bancquarts goodbye. The progression it makes through its phases is dependable and familiar; yet, as a pale shimmering body that drifts through the light of long-dead stars, it still feels elusive. In my efforts to capture its light long enough for a prolonged communion, I planted a moon garden, which has now matured into a wild space of all-white flowers in my backyard. Some, like primroses, bloom only by moonlight. Others bloom day and night nonstop: foxgloves, irises, violets, veronica, peonies, daisies, coneflowers, phlox, alyssum. Still others, namely, daylilies, live out their lives one lightning-quick bloom at a time. On nights of the full moon, the whole garden glows as if from a light source rising up through their roots.

I situated my writing desk to overlook the garden from my study. When I look out through the window at night, I see my face faintly reflected in the glass. When raindrops dapple the pane, my face scatters into multiple me's across my view of the garden. Moments and memories conflate into an infinite field of folding reflections. Recollections of my time with Marie-Claire rise to the surface: her astonishing intelligence and preternatural gift with language. The way she raised her chin slightly when she laughed. Her enigmatic cat. Her mythological take on everyday life and the everyday life that manifested her take on mythology. I remember her recollection of the way her poem "Icarus" came to her through the airwaves one night: she was watching a documentary about the recent discovery of a male corpse in the Tyrolean Alps. Scientists were unable to date the body at first, but eventually traced it back 5,000 years to the early Copper Age. Found alongside the body were artifacts, including a bow and quiver of arrows, an ax, a dagger, two wood vessels wrapped in maple leaves, and fur and leather garments.

"Voilà Icare!" she'd said. "That's Icarus!"

Icare

Étendu devant nous, congelé, il porte ce chiffre moyen :
l'homme.

On ne le date pas davantage.

Autour de lui herbes et plumes
témoignent pour un temps hors-temps.

Son ombre
mince chose cérémonielle
affirme une communauté d'exil.

Il chassait le renne
ou
plus fragile encore
le char d'assaut.

Qu'importe ?

Sa vie nue
décortiquée de ses espoirs par la bouche de la montagne
prend espace.

— Espace ?

— Solitaire
avec un élan vers Celui qui ne peut pas être
en ses fatigues et lieux nuls.

*

Il marche sur l'asphalte du dedans.

Comme un enfant de guerre extasié devant une orange
il s'éblouit devant le plus mince bonheur :
l'ardoise en place sur son toit,
le geste des statues qui serrent
leur poignée d'air.

Petits squares, territoires étroits de survie
son chemin d'intérieur ne les relie jamais.

Il pose une paume ouverte,
puis une autre :
— Viens, Dieu le grand oiseau !

Et Dieu s'envole après avoir piqué sa miette.

*

Mordu par la vastitude des voyages
ensanglanté de mots qui n'ont aucun cours dans son âme
il arpente la nuit.

Tout au fond du sommeil
son gisant
voit les reflets massifs de sa fièvre
en cathédrales, minarets, sales maisons des ports.

*

Au grenier qui vieillit, avec ses épis d'âme,
les nuits rongent dieux et oracles.

Le Christ défait la Croix en arbre mort.

La Sibylle mange tous les messages.

Vermoulu de ses rêves
à son tour
Icare est usé.

La suie solide des villes maudites
s'infiltre dans sa peau et ses os, très petits, bientôt nuls.

*

Après le cauchemar
il voit sur sa paume
trace de feuilles
leur insistance brune aux nervures, à la tige.

Il aimerait les repiquer sur son vieux corps volant.

*

Parfois tombe au printemps dans la dispersion de la pluie
une pluie plus serrée

comme de l'eau à vif
à l'heure où se taisent les rues.

Au-delà des averses lui apparaît le ciel sédentaire
avec les astres que voyait Virgile.

Il n'a pas avancé dans le déchiffrement des visages.

Il reste toujours sous l'absence.

Graine inéclose, bête seule
entre la fluorescence de la ville et le monde étoilé.

*

Son espoir
il le ramasse en lui.

Dans une grande forme de Pâques
il fait cuire son existence.

Le couteau pénètre.

Les fragments sont ensalivés, mâchés.

Minuscules restes du gâteau, petite nourriture d'univers,
il les roule doucement sur la paume, il y devine une
âme
enfin dissoute de bonheur, sauvage avec les graviers du jardin.

*

Serré
Son cœur sans ailes ?

— La cigale crie dans le périssable
à l'étroit.

Mais l'éternité du silence est brisée par son chant
préparant, prolongeant l'odeur des romarins sous les arbres.

Qui procéderait à la désignation du soleil
sinon ce bruit sur le ventre,
sec ?

*

Sans ailes.
Son cœur aura remise de sa peine
sur une route
un jour d'été
parmi les tôles froissées, les odeurs d'essence

ou sur une route
dans les blés fraîchement coupés qui piquent la peau
insensible.

Une tendresse lui viendra du moteur en morceaux
du chaume.

*

Près de lui tombe
en silence
l'oiseau.

Plus que jamais Icare ouvre les yeux sur la terre,
très rousse.

Il prépare sa venue dans la rose anglaise.

Ce qui le conduisait loin des caravanes horizontales
ce n'était pas la poussière des astres,
mais son cœur, qui battait sur l'énigme.

Maintenant
l'énigme est sa demeure ouverte.

Icarus

Stretched out before us, frozen, he fits an ordinary mold:
man.

We don't date him beyond that.

Around him grasses and feathers
attest to a time outside of time.

His shadow
thin ceremonial thing
confirms a community of exile.

He hunted reindeer
or
more fragile still
the battle tank.

What does it matter?

His bare life
husked of all hope by the mountain's mouth
takes up space.

—Space?

—Solitary
with an impulse toward One who can't coexist
with his exhaustion and emptiness.

*

He walks the pavement within.

Like a war orphan ecstatic over an orange
he's dazzled by the slightest pleasure:
the secure roof slate,
a statue's steadfast grip
on its handful of air.

Little patches; scant enclaves of survival
that his inner path never networked.

He lifts one open palm,
then the other
—Come, God the great bird!

And God flies off after pecking his crumb.

*

Struck by the vastness of voyages
bloodied by words that have no bearing on his soul
he paces the night.

In the depths of sleep
his recumbent figure
sees reflections of his fever amplified
in cathedrals, minarets, filthy harbor houses.

*

In the aging granary, with its cobs of soul,
Night gnaws on gods and oracles.

Christ dismantles the Cross into a dead tree.

The Sibyl eats all the messages.

Festering from his dreams
in turn
Icarus is sapped.

Cursed cities' crusted soot
infiltrates his skin and bones, so small, soon null.

∗

After the nightmare
he sees on his palm
leaf imprints
their brown insistence on the veins, on the stem.

He'd like to graft them onto his old flying body.

∗

Sometimes with springtime's dispersal of rain
falls a denser rain.

Like trickling water
the hour streets go silent.

Beyond the downpours he sees the sedentary sky
strewn with the same stars Virgil saw.

He still can't decipher faces.

He remains absent.

Unsprung seed, solitary beast
between the city's fluorescence and the starry world.

∗

His hope
is gathered within himself.

In a big Easter cake pan
he bakes his existence.

The knife penetrates.

The pieces are saliva-soaked, chewed up.

Minuscule cake crumbs, cosmic nibbles,
he rolls them gently around his palm, he divines one
soul
dissolved at last into joy, wild with the garden's gravel.

∗

Tight
his heart without wings?

—The cicada sings in the perishable
constriction.

Its song breaks eternity's silence
preparing, prolonging the scent of rosemary under the trees.

Who would proceed toward the designation of the sun
if not this sound scraping the stomach,
dry?

*

Without wings.
His heart will have healed from the pain
on a street
one summer's day
among the crumpled sheet metal and gasoline smell

or on a street
in the freshly cut wheat that stings the numb
skin.

A tenderness will come to him from the engine in pieces
of stubble.

*

Near him falls
in silence
the bird.

Wider than ever before Icarus opens his eyes over the earth,
deep red.

He prepares his arrival in the English rose.

What led him away from the horizontal caravans
wasn't stardust,
but his heart, which beat against the enigma.

Now
the enigma is his open dwelling.

Bear in Hibernation

by C. Cook

Tree roots reach
through a thicket
of fur
      into the glacially
slow heartbeat
of a bear, solitary

beast buried barely
alive in frozen soil.

Root threads reach
bear's dream of rising
and see her vision:
sweet viscous lift
of sap up the trunk,

each ligneous
        capillary
an open
        canal lock.

Sap lifts her heft higher,
quickens her pulse up the maple,

which awakens
an impulse
    to thaw.

Tree's ursine
      hunger urges

bear's almost arboreal
urge to reach for the sun.

THE ENGLISH ROSE ARRIVES each June, blooming crimson amidst my all-white moon garden. Its flowers are fragrant and full, the size of ripe pomegranates. I've seen bees enter the folds of a bloom only to exit, days later, drenched with pollen potent enough to pulse a poet back to life.

It is her heart, beating against the enigma.

Anise and Rosemary

by C. Cook

For Marie-Claire Bancquart

Every morning, the same:
birds land in my limbs.

Evenings, and cattle come
graze at my feet in the lessening

light. They tear at you
placidly, tasting anise

and rosemary, your
peppery leaves. My skin

lets light through to you. I am
your peat and humus, your dark

and your light.
A fruition.

NOTES

PROLOGUE

1. (p. 21) A dialogue that brings to mind philosopher Julia Kristeva's ruminations on the silent exchanges between a pregnant woman and the baby in her womb.

2. (p. 21) *The Art of Cinema*, Jean Cocteau (Marion Boyars Publishers Ltd, 1994; reprinted 2001), p. 156

3. (p. 25) Marie-Claire Bancquart, *Rituel d'emportement: Poèmes. 1969–2001* (Obsidiane & Le temps qu'il fait, 2002), p. 9. *Rituel d'emportement* is a book of Bancquart's selected poems.

4. (p. 25) *A Child's Book of Poems*, Gyo Fujikawa (Grosset & Dunlap, 1969)

5. (p. 33) *Rituel,* p. 11

CHAPTER THREE

6. (p. 85) *Rituel*, p. 9

CHAPTER FIVE

7. (p. 115) Alain Bancquart, "Doubles (La collaboration entre poète et musician)" in À *la voix de Marie-Claire Bancquart* (ed. Aude Préta-de Beaufort et Pierre Brunel, Cherche Midi, 1996)

CHAPTER SIX

8. (p. 133) Like most Westerners, I equate plainsong music with Gregorian chant, sung *a cappella* by hooded monks whose bass voices reverberate through damp candlelit cathedrals. Despite the genre's enduring medieval flavor, it is deeply rooted in the Ancient Greek *harmoniai*, which fell under the purview of Harmonia, the goddess of harmony and balance.

9. (p. 135) Saint Lazare Station, the first train station in Paris, built in 1837. It fascinated many Impressionist painters, most famously

Claude Monet, who painted it a dozen times. He particularly liked to paint scenes of steam billowing profusely out the train engines. Whenever he wanted to paint such a scene, he asked his stationmaster friend to have one of the engineers fire up a steam engine. When Émile Zola saw some of these paintings, he was struck by Monet's ability to transform such a sooty, grimy scene into one of billowing beauty. It inspired him to write, in his novel *La Bête humaine* (which also features Saint Lazare Station): "that is where painting is today . . . our artists have to find poetry in train stations, the way their fathers found poetry in forests and rivers."

10. (p. 135) From *Les Illuminations* by Arthur Rimbaud. At sixteen, the Symbolist poet ran away from his home in Northern France to Paris, where he spent the next four years writing most all the poetry he'd ever publish and living a tempestuous Bohemian life fueled by absinthe, opium, hashish, and a volatile love affair with poet Paul Verlaine. When he was twenty, he gave up poetry for a series of entrepreneurial jobs in Africa and died seventeen years later, in 1891.

11. (p. 137) Paris has a long tragic history of anti-Semitic rioting, which reached a peak around the turn of the twentieth century. One of these episodes, the Dreyfus Affair—named for a falsely imprisoned Jewish military officer named Alfred Dreyfus—was triggered by the extremely high price of bread.

12. (p. 137) Saint-Paul Station is in Le Marais, whose large Jewish community was targeted by the Nazis during WWII. Behind the station is L'église St-Paul St-Louis, the church where Cosette and Marius marry in Victor Hugo's *Les Misérables*.

13. (p. 137) Gérard de Nerval is the pen name of writer, poet, and translator Gérard Labrunie. He often walked his pet lobster, Thibault, on a blue silk ribbon leash. One night in 1855 while wandering the Place du Châtelet, then a squalid warren of medieval alleys and crooked stairways, Nerval hung himself from a window grille. Remarking on the incident, Charles Baudelaire said that Nerval "delivered his soul in the darkest street he could find."

14. (p. 139) Paolo Veronese's sixteenth-century *The Wedding Feast at Cana* depicts the Biblical scene where Jesus' divine identity is first revealed. At 22 feet high and 32 feet wide, it is the largest painting in the Louvre.

15. (p. 139) In his story "Unreal Cities," Nerval wrote: "We are entering the age of *Pracrit* (the vulgar tongue)—I became convinced of this while buying tickets for myself and my friend for the dance hall on rue St-Honoré, dubbed *Dance Hall of the Dogs* by those who can't afford to get in." (Richard Sieburth, trans.)

16. (p. 139) The suicide note Nerval left for his aunt read: "Don't wait up for me this evening, for the night will be black and white." Translator's note: a "white night" means a "sleepless night."

17. (p. 141) A traffic circle named after Charles X, the last Bourbon king of France. Charles X's hardline ultraroyalist perspective prevented him from understanding and, in the end, withstanding the strength of democratic spirit produced by the French Revolution.

18. (p. 141) "Right of wreck" refers to a medieval custom allowing landowners to seize whatever washed ashore from a shipwreck. Any wreck was considered an act of God punishing the crew for their sins. Therefore, the cargo could be—indeed, should be—claimed by those who owned the shore on which it landed.

19. (p. 141) Built in 1827, Pont de Grenelle collapsed and was rebuilt in 1874. That bridge collapsed and was rebuilt in 1968. A replica of the Statue of Liberty stands at one end.

20. (p. 141) 20,000 bulbs twinkle every night for five minutes on the hour until 1 a.m.

21. (p. 143) In 1920, l'Hôpital des Enfants Malades, the oldest children's hospital in the Western world, merged with Hôpital Necker, which was founded in 1778 by the mother of nineteenth-century writer Madame de Staël. Before the French Revolution, Hôpital Necker was L'Hospice de Charité, a Catholic hospital that required patients to present a baptismal certificate and say confession in order to receive care.

22. (p. 145) The Pillar of the Boatmen was erected in the 1st century CE by a guild of Gallic merchants to honor Jupiter, the paternal god of the Romans who'd recently conquered and colonized Gaul. The Pillar bears the Roman figures of Castor and Pollux as well as the Gallic gods Smertrios and Cernunnos, making it an extremely rare example of syncretism between the pantheon of the Romans and that of the Parisii, the indigenous Gallic tribe that lived along the banks of the Seine.

23. (p. 145) The Place de Grève is arguably the swampiest part of the Seine. Since the Roman times, it's been the site of festivals, political rallies, uprisings, and executions. One of the many people executed here was Catherine Monvoisin, known as "La Voisin." She was burned at the stake in 1680, accused of presiding over a sinister cabal of fortune tellers, palm readers, Tarotists, alchemists, witches, and sorcerers who provided potions, poisons, aphrodisiacs, and other magical services to their aristocratic clients. She was a midwife who performed whatever services her patients required, from births to abortions.

24. (p. 145) "Fold mountains" are mountains made from the crashing plates of Earth's colossal crust.

Acknowledgments

THERE ARE MANY LITERARY CANYONS in the United States, where fewer works-in-translation are published than in any other Western country. When I discovered how little of Marie-Claire Bancquart's work had been translated into English, I discovered just such a canyon in the canon of contemporary poetry: although Bancquart's work has been translated into nine languages, merely three of her thirty-plus books of award-winning poetry have been translated into English.

Thankfully, more and more literary journals and publishers are engaging in critical world-mending work to help non-Anglophile voices cross this country's borders. I'm grateful to the AIM Higher Board for including my translations and boundary-crossing narrative in their efforts to do just this, especially Executive Director Lissa Kiernan; Maureen Alsop, whose creative insights helped shape the book; and Kim Noriega, who brought it into exquisite fruition.

I am profoundly grateful, too, to Fiona Sze-Lorrain, who gave me invaluable feedback on the translations, poetry, and prose in this book; as well as Marcia LeBeau, whose yearslong support has nurtured my poet's soul. And to my husband, Jeff, and sons, Liam and Kieron: you are my inspiration.

I also extend my sincere appreciation to the French publishers of Marie-Claire Bancquart's books in which the following poems originally appeared:

"Au profond du corps," "S'éclate," "Du dimanche," "Du poète," "Millénaires," "Sans dresser d'ombre," "Embolie," "En toi," Été, "Farces et attrapes," "Mer ancienne," Depuis," "En échange," "Dans la bouche," "Intervalle," "Oui, l'intervalle," "Méconnue," "Bien le bonjour," "Mes os," "La parole des os," "Attifeur," "Terre," "Métamorphosés": Marie-Claire Bancquart, *Avec la mort, quartier d'orange entre les dents*, Éditions Obsidiane, 2005.

"Icare": Marie-Claire Bancquart, *Dans le feuilletage de la terre*, Éditions Belfond, 1994.

"Tarot": "I," "VIIII," "XV," "XXII": Marie-Claire Bancquart, *Partition*, Éditions Belfond, 1981.

"Femme": Marie-Claire Bancquart, *Mémoire d'abolie*, Éditions Belfond, 1978.

"Suite au dieu-lune," "Et contrefable d'Eurydice," "Intervalle": Marie-Claire Bancquart, *Opéra des Limites*, éditions Corti, 1988.

"Paris Plain-chant": Marie-Claire Bancquart, *Anamorphoses*, Écrits des Forges, 2003.

"V : Meurtre": Marie-Claire Bancquart, *Livre du Labyrinthe*, Mode Records, 2003.

So, too, do I extend my sincere appreciation to the editors of the publications in which the following poems and translations originally appeared, sometimes in earlier versions or under different titles:

Agenda Poetry: "Ancient Sea," "In the Mouth"
Cerise Press: "Bone-Speak"
Hayden's Ferry Review: "Slighted," "Of Sundays"
Poetry Salzburg Review: "Concerning the Poet," "Earth," "Joke"
Prairie Schooner: "Yes, the Interval"
Presence: "Anise and Rosemary"
Sugar Mule: "The Faith I Had in Death"
The Other Journal: "Tomatoes of Kobarid"
Third Coast: "Postmortem"
Unbound Press: "Driving Through Shrouds"
Words Without Borders: "My Bones," "Millennial"

My thanks, as well, to Karen Kelsay at Kelsay Books, publisher of my collection *A Strange Insomnia*, where the poems "Cell Block," "Anise and Rosemary," "The Faith I Had in Death," and "Postmortem" also appeared; and to the publishers of Cerise Press, where excerpts from my interview with Marie-Claire Bancquart first appeared, as well as *Hayden's Ferry Review* and *Words Without Borders*, whose blogs featured seedlings of this book in the form of my essays on translating and visiting Marie-Claire.

And last but certainly not least, I'm grateful to Cindy Hochman of "100 Proof" Copyediting Services for copyediting the English portions of the book—and grateful to Amanda Sarasien for copyediting the French portions. Their eagle eyes and poet's souls polished it to perfection.

About the Authors

CHRISTINA COOK is a poet, translator, book critic, and writer. Her first book, the poetry collection *A Strange Insomnia,* was preceded by two chapbooks, *Ricochet* and *Lake Effect,* the latter of which won the 2012 Jean Pedrick Chapbook Prize. Her work has been featured in literary journals across the US, Europe, and Australia. She has served as a speechwriter for presidents of Dartmouth College and the University of Pennsylvania, and has taught writing at several universities and colleges. Christina lives in State College, PA, where she practices astrology, Reiki, and Tarot. For more information and to contact Christina, please visit christinacook.us

MARIE-CLAIRE BANCQUART (1932–2019) was a prolific poet, novelist, essayist, and literary scholar. Over the course of her illustrious half-century career, she published dozens of books and received numerous awards for literary achievement, including France's most prestigious prizes for poetry and for scholarly work. Bancquart served as president of the French arts council La Maison de la Poésie, and after a long and fruitful teaching career, became a professor emerita of the Université Paris-Sorbonne in 1994. She lived in Paris with her husband, the internationally acclaimed composer Alain Bancquart.

About the Publisher

AIM Higher publishes books that blur boundaries, negate binaries, interrogate, confound, and delight. We endeavor to open portals into unmapped, magical dimensions, and hold deep respect for intuition and collaboration.

Also from AIM Higher

Lissa Kiernan   *The Whispering Wall*
Kim Noriega   *Naming the Roses*
Tina Barry   *I Tell Henrietta*

Colophon

Roaming the Labyrinth with Marie-Claire Bancquart is set in PS Fournier Standard, Grand, and Petit. Created by Stéphane Elbaz for Typofonderie, PS Fournier is designed in tribute to Pierre Simon Fournier (1712–1768), a prolific Parisian type designer whose work is best known for its iconic representation of French transitional style. PS Fournier elegantly represents the transition to the modern era of typography.